Next!

Next!

Auditioning for the Musical Theatre

Steven M. Alper

Cartoons by Herbert Knapp

Girandole **Books**
New York City

Girandole **Books**
590 West End Avenue
New York, New York 10024

We would like to thank those who have given their permission to include material in this book. Every effort has been made to contact the copyright holders for permission to reprint borrowed material where necessary. We regret any oversights that may have occurred and would be happy to rectify them in future printings of this work.

We wish to thank Heinemann for their assistance in the publishing of this reprint.

Cataloging-in-Publication Data
Alper, Steven M.
    Next!: auditioning for the musical theatre / by Steven M. Alper; cartoons by Herbert Knapp.
    Reprint. Originally published: 1st ed. Portsmouth, NH : Heinemann, 1995.

      p.   cm.
    Includes index.
    ISBN 978-0-997-16464-0
    1. Singing—Auditions. 2. Musicals—Auditions. I. Title.
MT892.A46 1995
792.6'028—dc20

Library of Congress Control Number: 2012937555

Editor: Lisa Barnett
Production: J. B. Tranchemontagne
Cover design: Phil Augusta

Printed in the United States of America

*This book is dedicated to all those who ever have or will have
a horror story to tell about an audition*

*and to the memory of casting director Joe Abaldo,
who went out of his way to keep there from being
any horror stories to tell.*

Contents

Acknowledgments

*T*here are those to whom I am indebted for their contribution to the creation of this book. I am forever grateful to all of them for their support, encouragement, and friendship.

Thanks go to my dear friends Dan Nani of Nani-Saperstein Management, Douglas Coates, Laurent "Spud" Giroux, Elizabeth Howell, Reneè Guerin, Christiane McKenna (whose blue pencil went beyond the call of duty), Noble Shropshire, Eliza Ventura (who always left me feeling encouraged), Marcia Milgrom-Dodge, and my agent, Helen Merrill.

And I deeply appreciate the contributions of Heinemann's Lisa Barnett, whose casting of the net dragged in this book, and J. B. Tranchemontagne for fitting all the pieces together; Frank Ventura of Collaborative Arts Project 21, for his suggestions for the chapter on types of auditions and for hoodwinking me into the classroom; Jerry Cole of the AEA, for providing answers and acting as a guide through the nearly inscrutable Equity audition codes; Hal and Peggy Serra, for providing more information than anyone could ever want to know about the history of chord symbols; Douglas Besterman, for checking the math, and for playing the other parts, too; all of my students at MTW

Conservatory, NYU-Tisch, and Collaborative Arts Project 21 over the years who listened, questioned, and challenged, and especially my very first class of Seniors; and all those who wittingly or unwittingly provided the horror stories told in this book.

And so very many thanks—a veritable "sign-up list for ten days of open calls worth of thanks"—go to Herb Knapp, whose FABulous cartoons have contributed so much; and to my personal, in-house, pre-editor, Mary Knapp, who constantly kept me from wandering astray. I doubt this book could have existed without them.

And most of all, I thank Sarah, who told me I could do it.

Introduction

*I*t has often been said that acting cannot be taught. However, most of you who will read this book currently are, have been, or will be paying someone somewhere a lot of money *to be taught to act*. What you will get for your money is not the secret of great acting, but hopefully, the tools you will need to become a great actor, as well as the basic skills and processes on which to graft your own individuality in order to create something unique and marvelous.

In this book, I'll provide you with some of the tools you will need to give a successful musical audition. There will be a lot of basic "dos and don'ts," pitfalls you can avoid and rules that I feel you should never break, along with a lot of suggestions or nudges that should give you some ideas on how to proceed on your own.

From first-year musical-theatre students auditioning to get into school to seasoned Broadway performers auditioning for their seventh Broadway show—I've seen it all. More than twenty years' experience watching auditions and watching other people watch auditions has provided me with the material to formulate certain theories that I am certain you will find useful. The next best thing to actually sitting behind the table and watching the auditions is the information you'll find in this book.

We'll start with basics, the stuff you'll need to have, need to do, and need to know. Stuff about which there can be no argument: how to prepare your music, how to find your music, how to prepare for auditions, etc. We'll also look at the more iffy stuff, where I'll be saying, "Well, I think tomato, but this other guy thinks definitely and exclusively, to*MAH*to."

Interspersed will be some humorous illustrations, examples, and a large number of anecdotes from people on both sides of the casting table that will portray failures and successes, interesting attempts, and sketches of the types of characters you will come up against.

You will also meet my wife, actress Sarah Knapp, whose audition experiences will be shared as useful illustrations for certain points. (A student in one of my audition classes said that sometimes she thought Sarah was teaching the class more than I was!)

What you'll get from all this is a springboard. After reading this book, you should be able to take the information and use it to showcase and develop your unique self at auditions. Every audition you attend will be like a conversation with someone who has something you want, including the information you need in order to be more valuable in their eyes. It is a real free-for-all, and you'll have to play each and every audition by ear because shows are made by people, and each person has his own twisted, precious view of the world (you included, I hope).

"Today I would like to sing..."

"You brought *THAT?!!!* AHAHAHAHAhahahahahahahahahahahahahaha..."

The Audition— The What, the Why, and the When

1

"*T*he play's the thing" according to Hamlet, but without the involvement of actors, it's not much: a slew of words in a script, some notes on manuscript paper, maybe a lighting plot and some sketches. The creators of the most brilliant musical ever written have no way to communicate its brilliance without actors to reveal it. There are many points in the genesis of a piece at which the use of real, living actors becomes not just useful but necessary.

A Show Is Born!

So, somebody's written this fabulous show—it's smash-o, sock-o, killer. Let's say it's *Boffo—A New Musical*, with music by Esther Spelling, lyrics by Steven Scott, and book by Leo Jules. They've spent six years on this project to date, and now, after the eighteenth draft (*draft* being the term used for a major revision), the creators feel that it's finally time to let people see what they've done.

The first order of business is to get the script into a readable form. Next, since the show *is* a musical, there's got to be a way to demonstrate to potentially interested

1

parties what the music sounds like. Sending some sheet music along with the script is probably not the best way to get the score across, so they decide to make a demonstration recording, or *demo*, of the songs. Since neither Leo nor Steven can carry a tune—and since Esther is notoriously temperamental in the recording studio—they've decided to bring in a group of actors in order to get the best-quality recording they can.

This is one of the first phases in the development of a new musical in which actors may begin to contribute. At this point auditions are rarely called for. Because there is usually little or no money for salaries, the creators will generally call in some actors they have had some previous relationship with.[1]

Once the demo has been recorded (and this one for *Boffo* is just *FABulous*, let me tell you!), the creators blitzkrieg the postal routes. Hundreds of copies of the script and demo are sent out to producers and theatre companies all over the country. And the team is lucky enough to get an immediate bite! A hotshot Broadway producer, Max A. Millyon, contacts them to express his interest.

The creators are beside themselves. Mr. Millyon, although completely cognizant of his own impeccable taste and ability to pick a potential hit, wants to put together a very *informal reading* of the piece: "just to get an idea of how it plays," he says.

Several of the actors who performed on the demo are brought together with a group of additional people (some of them are not even performers, just friends of friends) in Mr. Millyon's living room to do a *cold reading* (an unprepared, or only slightly prepared read-through of the script—although, let's face it, with so much riding on this, they don't want to blow their chances with Max, so the actors who will be singing some of the bigger songs are *thoroughly* rehearsed).

This reading is an enormous success ("It reads good!" says Mr. Millyon). Mace Ihvego, who has directed many of Max's hits, attended the reading and agrees with Max's assessment, but feels that the show could benefit from a workshop.

The term *workshop* is used to describe a variety of different types of rehearsal processes, but all of them exist in order to give bookwriter(s), lyricist(s), and composer(s) (sometimes with the addition of the creative team—the director, musical director,

---

1. Although all of the unions have rules regarding demo recordings, they generally have turned a blind eye to the participation of their performers (unless the production is particularly lavish—say, with a full orchestra), realizing that the creation of new work can benefit their membership in the long run, with productions, replacement casts, tours, cast recordings, etc. (But don't tell 'em I said so . . .)

choreographer—and even the producers) the time to do some thorough tinkering. There are several groups around the country who specifically and exclusively exist to create this kind of opportunity (the O'Neill Theater Center, the Sundance Institute, and The New Harmony Project, among others). And many theatre companies, especially developmental theatre companies, produce workshops as well (that's what *developmental* means).

What occurs during a workshop will depend on the ultimate goals of the writers and the producing organization. Basically, in a workshop actors spend some time working on a piece or a portion of a piece (maybe just an act or scene that is not working as effectively as the creators would like). The creators come in, watch the actors working, and go away to rewrite. Then the actors work with the revised material. This may be repeated *ad infinitum*. The process may culminate in some kind of public performance—or it may not.

The best course of action (as decided by Mr. Millyon) is to put together a privately funded workshop. The workshop will last a month *in toto*, and will be broken down into two weeks of rehearsal followed by three days of performances, another week of rehearsal, and then three final days of performance. This will allow the writers to rework material during the first rehearsal period, and then have a chance to see what happens when the show is put in front of an audience. Based on audience response and feedback from the performers, the writers will have another full week of rehearsal in which to rewrite. Then there is the final group of performances, when the writers will have a chance to see how their latest set of changes work (and then, of course, respond with another series of rewrites).

Several new talents will be added to the brew for this workshop:

- Dennis Dirigent, a musical director, brought in to teach the music; help with vocal arrangements (harmonies) and piano arrangements; play rehearsals and performances; and advise and assist the writers based on his knowledge of performance practice (and innate good taste);
- A rehearsal pianist, for those times when the musical director needs to be in two places at once;
- A stage manager, to help keep things under control, people at rehearsal, rehearsal spaces booked, and schedules maintained;
- Tepdan Skidd, the choreographer (in a strictly advisory position), to collaborate with the director and help with the staging.

And overseeing it all, of course, will be Max's good friend and director, Mace Ihvego. It will be his job to see that the workshop has some kind of value, that unclear moments become clarified, that flabby moments are trimmed, and that the line of the piece (its flow and direction) is maintained—in other words, that some growth occurs. Because the emphasis of a workshop is on the enhancement of the script, not on the physical production (sets, lighting, costumes, staging, even actors are secondary), and because time will be at a premium, he will make sure that any (necessarily) rudimentary staging is done solely to reinforce and assist the telling of the story. Of course he will also inspire, provoke, and give direction to the actors.

The authors originally intended for the cast of *Boffo* to be fairly large—twenty-four—but in order to save money on salaries, it is decided to *double* as often as possible. (Some actors will be playing more than one role.) In this way they manage to reduce the total number of actors needed to fourteen. Of the actors who performed in the original informal reading, five are asked to participate in the workshop (well, six, actually, but one of them has a prior commitment that compels her to decline) and auditions are scheduled to fill the other nine spots.

Because an actor's contribution to a piece during a workshop can conceivably be substantial, Actors' Equity will often require that the *Right of First Refusal* be made a part of an actor's workshop contract. Basically what this means is that in the event of a full production of the show within a certain amount of time (it varies with the contract), the actor either has to be offered the role in the subsequent production, or *bought out* of the contract—that is, paid an amount equal to the salary for a specific number of weeks on the new contract (this figure also varies per contract). Since the salary for workshops is generally pretty modest, this Right of First Refusal can often make the prospect of doing a workshop more appealing to an actor.

The workshop, unfortunately, is a disaster. Mr. Ihvego loses touch with the goals of the project and wastes time with endless staging and restaging of scenes, and dealing with the unnecessary and excessive use of props. He spends an inordinate amount of time in senseless, meaningless discussions with the actors about acting methods. The writers bicker among themselves and chase pointless plot lines down blind alleys—generally writing themselves into corners. Worst of all is Esther Spelling, who is totally intractable, refusing to make any kind of changes whatsoever. She says, "I've done my work! You make your changes around my music!" By the final performance, Max Millyon's utter contempt for the music and its composer provokes him to withdraw from the project.

And so *Boffo* dies from lack of interest. (You could say that a promising piece met its end because of a Ms. Spelling.)

Well, but Anyway . . .

Let's take a look at some of the other steps that may occur in the development of a theatrical piece.

- A more formal type of reading is the *staged reading*. In this kind of performance there will be minimal staging, and the actors will (usually) perform with scripts in hand. Only a certain number of hours of rehearsal are permitted by Equity, and payment to the performers is negligible.
- Sometimes when a piece cannot gain sufficient financial backing for a full production to be mounted, the people behind the project may produce what in New York City is called a *showcase production*. In Los Angeles it's called an *Equity Waiver Production*. This type of production is often done in the hopes of gaining some attention for the piece in order to make the project more attractive to investors. A showcase or waiver production is (usually) mounted with a minimal set, lighting, costume, and advertising budget, in a relatively small space, for a limited run. The actors may be paid as little as carfare.
- In earlier days, the creators of a piece (often with the addition of several professional actors) would do a kind of informal presentation of excerpts from a piece for potential investors. This was known as a *backers' audition* and was performed in a more casual setting, such as someone's apartment, and for a relatively small audience. The composer would sit at the piano, the lyricist and bookwriter out front describing the action and everyone singing. Very often there would be an abundance of food, and the potential backers would be plied with liquor in the hope that this would provide the necessary lubricant to help extract funds from their wallets. By agreement with Equity, there are limits to the number of hours allowed for rehearsal, and the actors receive a small stipend.

  Although this practice has not disappeared entirely, nowadays a public staged or informal reading may be referred to as a backers' audition when performed for potential investors.

- Similar to backers' auditions are *theatre party presentations*. These presentations are given for salespeople and leaders of theatre party groups, whose purchases of tickets in blocks make up a large percentage of the gargantuan advance ticket sales reported for some Broadway shows. The presentations are much more like the original backers' audition in that a selection of excerpts from the piece is performed with narration in place of most of the dialogue, and food is served, but they are done on a much larger scale, sometimes in a Broadway house for audiences of thousands.

Into Production

After all of this knocking about, hopefully a piece will have been massaged into good enough condition for someone to decide that it is ready to see light as a full production. The most prestigious of these (in the U.S., anyway) is a Broadway production.

Traditionally, before a show would be mounted in a Broadway theatre, it would be subjected to an out-of-town tryout. The entire production—sets, lights, costumes, actors, and all—would be moved from city to city, up and down the eastern seaboard, undergoing changes and (hopefully) improvements along the way. And at the end of this major schlep was the glory of a New York opening—after which, depending on the fancies of whichever Fate was in charge of reviews and the whims of word-of-mouth at the moment, the show would either ride out into the sunset of national tours and regional and amateur community theatre productions, or simply sink into oblivion as a mere footnote in books about more successful projects.

For a variety of reasons (not the least of which is the fact that producing a flop has become more expensive than ever before), various other routes have become popular as a means of bringing a show to its pinnacle—with stops along these routes sometimes proving to be pinnacles in themselves.[2] In the old days, once a show had been successful on Broadway it would spawn a legion of national tours; nowadays the national tour may

2. *Phantom*, with a book by Arthur Kopit, and music and lyrics by Maury Yeston, is one of the most performed and financially successful shows of recent years. But although it has seen a national tour and has become a staple of stock and regional theatres, it has never been on Broadway. (In case you hadn't heard, there is a show with a similar name, with music by Andrew Lloyd Webber, which has had a successful run on Broadway.)

"Now, children, I know that we're just performing for the other first-grade classes right now, but our principal, Mr. Blemblicker, assures me that a group of backers is coming in to see the show, so a move to Broadway is quite possible!"

precede the Broadway opening. (It's much safer to make a bundle out in the world and *then* lose it all when it opens in New York!) Or a group of regional theatres may decide to form an alliance to finance a kind of minitour between each of their theatres with the intent of raising capital and finding the additional resources needed to move the piece to Broadway. Or a show may be initially mounted at a single regional or stock theatre with or without the intent of moving it elsewhere—although the creators and performers are usually hoping that a move will occur, somehow. When there is a planned attempt to move the show to another theatre, it is often with added funding support supplied by outside backers. (As a matter of fact, you are bound to hear the whispered rumor, "We're moving to Broadway, maybe . . ." in almost every show you do nowadays—whether it's a three-million-dollar regional production of a new musical by Alan Menken, or a non-Equity dinner theatre production of *Dames at Sea* in Tampa, Florida!)

The actual designation of the many types of venues and productions is determined by agreement with the Actors' Equity Association—the theatrical actors' union.[3] In the early days, whether a show was on the road, on Broadway, or playing a limited engagement in Aunt Alma's attic, if there was a contract with Equity it was a Production contract. In the 1950s, Equity was finding that stock productions had their own set of peculiarities and needs, and so came up with a new variation of contract specifically worded to meet these needs. When a production's requirements are such that no existing contract will fit, it is still possible to make a deal with Equity. Since it is Equity's desire to have the greatest number of its members working (under reasonable working conditions, of course), they are willing to negotiate special contracts, known as *Letters of Agreement*, or LOAs. When Equity finds consistencies within LOAs, they will create a new contract category. And thus we have the rather bewildering variety of contracts, all derived from the original Production contract.

As we've seen, there are the Workshop and Showcase (or Waiver) contracts. In addition, there are the many different stock and regional theatre contracts. There is not much apparent difference between stock and regional theatres (regional theatres tend more often to be not-for-profit), but each has a diversity of

---

3. There are, of course, other unions which handle other forms of theatrical performances, such as dance and opera, but let's leave that for someone else's book.

contracts based on the size of house, the length of run, the price of tickets, etc.

Then there are the Production contracts. National (or First-Class) tours, Bus and Truck tours, and pre-Broadway tours are all covered by this kind of contract. All three have the same base level of salary. What distinguishes the different types of tours is the length of stay in each city and the amount of rehearsal permitted. A production may play a town for months on a national tour; a Bus and Truck may be scheduled for one-nighters; and a pre-Broadway tour may allow additional hours of rehearsal (since the show is essentially under development).

In addition to the "touring" Production contracts, there is a "stationary" Production contract. This has the most cachet, the one you get when you've made it big, the one you get when you're on Broadway (and in some of the larger houses around the country). As in any other Production contract, however, the base salary is the same.

Getting In

Once upon a time, a young performer trying to get into an Equity audition would be trapped in a vicious cycle: in order to audition for an Equity show, you would have to be a member of Equity, but you couldn't become a member of Equity without being in an Equity show! Many people found their way into Equity by being cast in a non-Equity show that became an Equity production; being requested to audition for an Equity show despite their non-Equity status; being cast in an Equity show in a city or town with a relatively small Equity population; or going through a lengthy Equity Candidacy Program where they would serve for several years doing menial apprentice labor on Equity productions.

In recent years the rules of the game have changed, and now the requirements make it easier for non-Equity actors to get into Equity auditions (although it's still pretty hard to get into an Equity show). No longer is showing your Equity card a necessity for gaining entrance to the audition; now you can show an Equity Eligibility card and they'll let you in. In order to gain eligibility, an actor must prove a certain amount of experience and success as a performer. This is usually determined by proving a certain level of earnings derived from performing. (An Equity spokesman told me that there are a significant number of Equity members who do not meet the eligibility requirements and are therefore ineligible for Equity auditions!)[4]

Get Along, Little Dogie

Beginning actors will find that getting into a non-Equity audition is not anywhere near as daunting a prospect as getting into an Equity audition. Non-Equity producers are not constrained by any particular set of rules and may establish any type of requirements and conventions they'd like (hopefully remaining within the labor laws of the United States). A set of auditions is called an *open call* when either the call is not required by Equity, or the producer has no agreement with Equity (a non-Equity production). Open calls are often referred to as "cattle calls," and once you've experienced one, you realize why. The way actors are herded about in an open call is definitely reminiscent of "a big roundup"—the big differences being that hog-tieing is not allowed and the mooing and lowing have slightly more variety.

In contrast, the Equity audition procedures have been tailored over the ages to become efficient at enabling casting people to see huge numbers of people in a short period of time, while allowing the auditioning actors to retain a modicum of dignity. And in most contracts made between a producer and Actors' Equity, the producer is required to see a certain minimum number of auditioning actors (another number which varies based on the contract).

Since most non-Equity auditions and even open calls are ultimately based on the Equity models, I will confine the discussion to the Equity varieties. (Be aware that the rules and policies of Equity change frequently enough that you should occasionally check for what is currently in force.)

The EPA

Nope, this has nothing to do with the Environmental Protection Agency. Or even to what was, in days of yore, called the Equity

---

4. For more detailed information about Equity Eligibility requirements, send a self-addressed, stamped envelope along with your request to: Actors' Equity Association,165 W. 46th St., New York, NY 10036, attn: Eligibility.

Principal Audition. The EPA, as we will discuss it here, refers to an outgrowth of the original Equity Principal Audition: the *Eligible Performer Principal Audition*. (Yes, I know there are more *p*'s in the name than in the acronym; that's just the way it is!) At the EPAs the auditors are seeking to cast principal or leading roles.[5]

On each day of an EPA, one hour before auditions are scheduled to begin, a numbered sign-up sheet will be posted by the monitor outside of the audition room.[6] Once the sign-up sheet has been filled, the monitor will read off, in order, the names on the list. As each name is called, the actor (after proving eligibility) comes forward and chooses an audition appointment from a list of available time slots. The list shows the day broken up into three- or four-minute segments (depending on how many actors the producer is required to see). The actor is then issued a card with that time on it. He must then appear ready to audition fifteen minutes prior to the time on the card. At this point, as long as you've stuck to the rules, you are guaranteed to be seen—even if they're ahead of schedule and you could have been seen hours earlier. (Of course, if they're running *behind*, you'll have to wait for your turn.)[7]

After all of the time slots have been filled, an *open-ended alternate list* will be created. This list is posted for the duration of the call, and actors may add their names to this list at any time during the call. From this list, and in the order that the names have been signed, the monitor will call actors to fill in the gaps created due to actors' absences at the time of their scheduled

---

5. You may hear occasional mention of *Eligible Performer Principal Interviews*. There was a time when actors, instead of actually auditioning, would be interviewed by the producers of a show to give a sense of how the actor might contribute to the production—this interview usually followed by a callback audition. Nowadays, EPIs are rarely held, if ever.

6. Actors who have arrived prior to the appearance of the monitor and the official sign-up sheet may agree to create an "unofficial" one. Equity does not acknowledge the validity of these lists, so there is no way that use of the list can be enforced. Note that the Actors' Equity building in New York opens at 8:00 A.M., and actors arriving for an EPA will, as a practice, take a seat in front of the list in the order in which they arrived.

7. As of this writing, Actors' Equity has temporarily agreed to test a different scheduling arrangement. Rather than break the call into a three- or four-minute segment per actor, the call will be broken down into twenty-minute blocks. Six actors will be scheduled within each block, the length of each audition to be determined by the casting director (but never less than one minute). Any time left over in a block will be given to actors appearing on the alternate list. This should not affect actors too much, but if you're concerned, contact Equity to find out what procedure is currently being enforced.

appointment or due to auditions running ahead of schedule. And those same actors who missed their appointments (thus allowing some lucky alternates to get in!) may add their names to the bottom of the alternate list. Unfortunately, the appearance of your name on the alternate list is not a guarantee of being seen. However, at the end of the call, the monitor will pass on the pictures and resumes of the actors whose names appeared on the alternate sheet and weren't seen.

How early people start arriving for these calls depends on the appeal of the production and what time the building opens (and it's not unheard of for actors to begin lining up outside of the building even before it opens). Assuming that you have arrived early enough to get a good choice of appointment times, you'll have to give some thought to appropriate battle tactics. Some people (especially those who live far away from the audition site) feel that it's best to choose the earliest appointment, just to get it over with. Others show up all sloppy and unmade-up, pick a later time and go home to wake up, freshen up, make up, and warm up (especially those who live nearby or those who prefer not to sing first thing in the morning).

Chorus Calls

For *Eligible Performer Chorus Calls* (auditions exclusively for non-leading roles), a sign-up sheet is posted at Actors' Equity at 9:30 A.M., one week prior to the auditions. Immediately after the sheet appears, a line will usually form in front of it. Only one signature is permitted for each trip through the line, so if an actor is planning to sign up some friends, he must go back to the end of the line for each name he intends to add to the list. The list is taken down at 5:00 P.M. on the day before the auditions.

A half hour before auditions are scheduled to begin, the actors are called in the order in which they have signed up. If you fail to respond when your number is called, you lose (Do not pass go. Do not collect $200). Then the monitor, still in the order of the sign-up list, will distribute *Chorus Call Audition Cards* to the actors. These cards are numbered sequentially, and actors at the beginning of the list receive the lower numbers.

You don't have to sign your name to the list during its one-week appearance at Equity. If you appear at the audition site while the distribution of the Chorus Cards is taking place (a half hour before the auditions), you can receive a card once all of the cards have been given out to those who *did* sign up. Actors who were not there when their names were called can also get cards at this point.

Outside of the audition room during the auditions, the monitor will have posted a listing with the names and titles of everyone involved with running the call. As the actor prepares to go into the audition room, the monitor is required to announce the current obligatory audition length. I say *current,* because the casting people are allowed to change this during the day—they can start a call, for instance, requiring thirty-two bars or less, and later on reduce this to sixteen bars. The monitor will also instruct the actor as to what the auditors expect to see from the performers in terms of song and monologue types.

And speaking of types . . . At the beginning (and only at the beginning) of a call, it is permissible for the casting people to bring all of the actors into the room at once and eliminate those who, for whatever reason, don't match the physical characteristics they imagine for the cast. This is known as *typecasting,* or simply, *typing.*

If you have received a card and are missing in action when they call you to audition, you don't get to audition (although if there's any time remaining at the end of the call, they may still see you). If you have received a card and would have been there when they called you if they had ever gotten around to calling you, but, no!, they spent so much time on everybody else that you just didn't get your chance—well, then they just have to reschedule you. You see, once you have your card and have followed all of the rules (including staying in the waiting area) and managed to get through the typing, you have a guarantee of being seen at some time.

By Appointment Auditions

At *By Appointment Auditions* the actor is treated less like a commodity than at EPAs. To begin with, an actor's presence is formally requested at By Appointment Auditions. Rather than signing up, an actor is given a specific audition time in advance. To select actors for the audition, the casting director may choose from his files, from requests made by the production team, from actors originally seen at an EPA, and from pictures and resumes solicited from agents and managers.[8] The casting director will then call the actor's agent, manager, or the actor directly to schedule an appointment. The casting director will also provide any pertinent details, i.e., what to prepare as far as monologues and songs go, information about the character the actor will be auditioning for, whether the actor will be asked to dance, rehearsal and performance schedules, and information about the production team. The casting director may also ask that the actor come in and pick up *sides* (short dialogue selections from the play or musical) or possibly even a song to prepare for the audition. On a new piece, the casting director may keep full copies of the script at his office for the actor to come in and read. It's usually only the bigger stars who are given a full script to peruse at their leisure.

When the actor arrives at the audition, he checks in with the monitor, and at approximately the time of the scheduled appointment (depending on how far behind things have gotten), he will be ushered into the room to give a glorious performance.

What Happens There

Once you enter the room, all *principal* (leading or featured roles) auditions are run pretty much according to the same plan. You'll be escorted in by the monitor and, after introducing yourself, you'll head straight over to the accompanist where you'll prepare to sing. Once you have sung, you'll be thanked and prompted to leave, or you may be asked to do your monologue(s) or to read from some sides. If you were given the sides in advance (either prior to audition, or when you first signed in for the audition), you either will be asked to read right away, or you may be asked to step out of the room until there is another actor to read with you.[9] If you've just been given the sides after you sing, you will either be given the time outside of the room to study the scene or asked to read it cold (see Figure 1).

Very seldom is an actor cast after a first audition. During most series of auditions, the casting people will gradually refine their

---

8. Do *not* call or send unsolicited pictures and resumes to casting directors on your own. It is not taken well and your photo will inevitably end up in the trash.

9. If you find out who you'll be reading with and have the time to do so while you're in the hall waiting to go back in, it's usually okay to rehearse the scene (quietly) with the other actor(s).

The Audition Flowchart

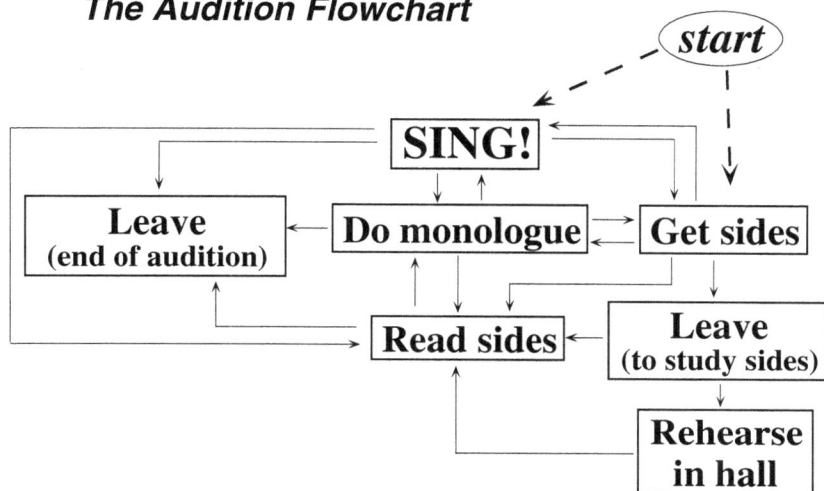

```
                                              start
                                                │
                                                ┆
                         ┌──── SING! ◄──────────┤
                         │     │ ▲              │
                         ▼     ▼ │              ▼   ▼
  ┌──────────────┐   ┌──────────────┐   ┌──────────────┐
  │    Leave     │◄──│ Do monologue │◄──│  Get sides   │
  │(end of audition)│ └──────────────┘   └──────────────┘
  └──────────────┘       ▲ │ │              │
         ▲               │ ▼ ▼              ▼
         │           ┌─────────────┐   ┌──────────────┐
         └──────────►│  Read sides │◄──│    Leave     │
                     └─────────────┘   │(to study sides)│
                            ▲          └──────────────┘
                            │                 ▼
                            │          ┌──────────────┐
                            └──────────│   Rehearse   │
                                       │   in hall    │
                                       └──────────────┘
```

Figure 1

choices by reducing the group being considered for each role. The smaller group is then brought back for one or more auditions until a casting decision is possible (see Figure 2).

By Appointment callbacks are usually scheduled through the casting director in the same way as the original audition. Calls are made to the agents, managers, or actors to schedule the appointment. Eligible Performer callbacks are often set up immediately following the audition ("Can you come back Tuesday at one?"). By Appointment callbacks may be set up this way as well. Callbacks may even be scheduled for the same day ("Could you come back this afternoon at 4:15?"). However the callback is scheduled, you should be told what to prepare; e.g., the same song, a different song, a song from the show, the same monologue, a different monologue, the same sides, or different sides.

The audition procedure at the callbacks will usually be the same as at an initial By Appointment Audition. (Yes, even callbacks from open calls may be by scheduled appointment—although a large number of people may be scheduled for the same time period.)

The Mirror and the Chance to . . .

At any time during this process, you may be asked to attend a dance audition.

THE CASTING SPREADSHEET						
	ROLE A	ROLE B	ROLE C	ROLE D	ROLE E	ROLE F
1st set of auditions						
1st Callback						
2nd Callback						
3rd Callback	*(director decides to play role himself)*					
Final Cast						

Figure 2

Whether part of a set of By Appointment Auditions or an *Eligible Performer Chorus Dance Call* (a series of auditions exclusively for dancers), dance calls are run in basically the same way. (For larger cast musicals, the dance auditions may be split into parts: one for dancers and one for actors who "move well."[10])

At the dance call, the actor/dancers are ushered into the audition space and allowed a few minutes to warm up. Then they are taught some choreography, sometimes several dance combinations of increasing difficulty. The choreography will usually reflect the style of the show, but the audition material may not actually be *from* the show.

Bear in mind that the choreographer may be allowing the input of members of the production team. For example:

The Director: Keep working with that big redhead. We need his type.

or

The Choreographer *(to the Director):* Watch her. I want you to see why I don't think she's right for us.

Once the actor/dancers have demonstrated their abilities sufficiently, a group may be eliminated. Then the steps may be run again, or some new, more difficult material may be added—

---

10. It's a good idea to be honest when asked by casting people about your dance skills. First of all, it'll be very obvious to everyone watching if you've lied about your abilities. Second, an actor who just "moves well" will come off much better auditioning in a group of "movers" than he would with a group of *dancers!*

The NEW Audition Flowchart

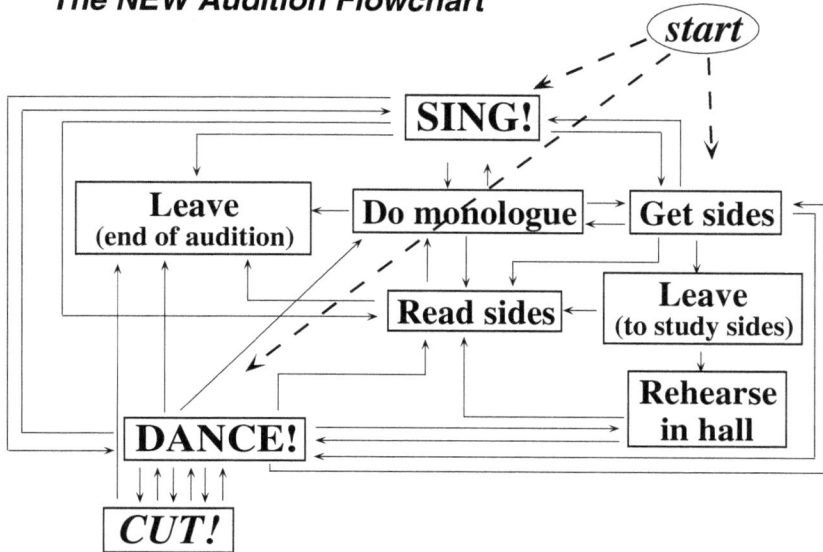

Figure 3

all leading up to another round of eliminations taking place. This may be repeated indefinitely until the group has been reduced to a final manageable number to select from for the ultimate casting. Remember the beginning of *A Chorus Line* where what appears to be about a million dancers are on the stage at once, all jostling for position and fighting to show off—and then, *cut!* half as many, and then *cut!* half again, and then *cut! cut! cut!* until the final small group is left (see Figure 3).

While for EPAs the dance call may be one of the last steps of the process, for open or Eligible Performer Chorus Dance Calls, the dancers are not asked to sing until after they have made the cut. They may or may not be given time after the dance call to change out of their dance clothes (usually dripping wet by now), before being led in to sing. When the dancers are asked to sing immediately after the dance call, the entire group is usually asked to wait. They are then called into the room one by one.[11]

It's possible, too, that rather than the line-up-to-sing-after-

---

11. Even though a dancer's singing ability is expected to be inversely proportional to his dancing ability (the better they dance, the less well they are expected to sing, and vice versa), a person who dances really well and sings really well is one of the most valuable people in the musical theatre. Don't expect to coast on your dancing skills alone (or else consider auditioning for a ballet company instead of the theatre).

the-cuts procedure just described, a dancer may be scheduled for a separate singing (and reading) callback. And it's not entirely unheard of for a person who came in for an open dance call to get called back to sing and read for a principal role at the By Appointment Callbacks.

Who's Who

There are quite a number of people you'll be bumping into at auditions. They will each have their own jobs and their own agendas. Here's some information about some of them.

- **The Monitor**, depending on the type of audition, is either an Equity member assigned by Equity or a person selected by the people holding the auditions. It is the monitor's job to see to it that people are signed in; that whatever additional information is needed by the production team or the actors is passed on to the relevant party; that the actors get into the room in the appropriate sequence; and that Equity's rules for the audition are followed. The monitor also helps keep things flowing smoothly in and out of the audition room—that is, actors, messages, and food deliveries.
- **The Writers** are the creators of the show—the bookwriter, the lyricist, and the composer. There may be any number of these, and the titles can be combined in many ways (e.g., bookwriter/lyricist). The writers' goals at the audition will be to fill each role with an actor who seems to best fit their idea of the character.
- **The Producer** is the money person, the financial backing behind the production. He may not be providing the actual cash himself, but will have been involved in getting it.

  At auditions for a theatre company, if a person is referred to as "a producer," he may be an *outside* producer—someone who is helping a particular production at this theatre with an infusion of cash in the hope that the production may be moveable to another venue (e.g., Broadway). Or he may be the person on the company's staff charged with overseeing and maintaining this production.
- **The General Manager** is the person hired by the production (or a member of the theatre company staff) to oversee the expenditure of funds. He helps draw up the budgets and makes sure they're stuck to. (My definition of "a really good

general manager" is someone you still like even while he's saying no.)

- **The Artistic Director** of a theatre company is its philosophical leader. He steers the direction of a company, determines what pieces are done in its season, defines the company's goals, and represents the theatre to the public. He oversees all aspects of the theatre's operation and is involved in raising funds for the company. He may also direct productions done by the company.

- **The Director** is responsible for the overall artistic integrity of a production. He provides the vision for a piece and makes sure that the rest of the creative staff and the actors stay within the bounds of that vision. He stages the show and guides the actors. At an audition, he will want to see that the auditioning actors demonstrate abilities that will allow decisions about casting to be made. Since he will be the one who ultimately spends the most time with the actors, and since his work depends almost entirely on the talents of the cast, he will want to make sure that the cast is composed of people he can work with and whose talents he can rely on.

- **The Choreographer** creates the dances for a show and may also help with the staging. At an audition, the choreographer will have some dance combinations prepared that will allow the actors to demonstrate any abilities that will be needed for the piece. (This material may not actually appear in the final production.)

- **The Musical Director** is responsible for the sound of the musical elements in a show. He will oversee the learning of the music, the creation of instrumental and vocal arrangements, and is likely to act as conductor for the performances. (Some shows have a separate **Conductor** who is brought in to replace the musical director once performances begin. He is usually responsible to the musical director.)

   At an audition, the musical director will bear in mind the requirements of each role, and may request specific or additional songs in order to help the actor demonstrate his ability to meet those requirements.

- **The Accompanist** is at an audition to play for the auditioning actors. (For much greater detail, see Chapter 3, "The Care and Feeding of the Piano Player.")

- **The Casting Director**'s job is to so thoroughly understand the requirements of the roles in a show that he can call in a selection of those actors who are most capable of fulfilling those requirements. Obviously, there is no way for a person to have knowledge of every living, eligible, and available actor—or even to be completely cognizant of the full extent of a *single* actor's talents. So casting directors will supplement the pool of actors with whom they are familiar by requesting submissions from agents and managers, and by posting advertisements in the theatrical trade papers. Since it is in the casting director's best interest to bring in only those actors who fit the needs of a production (the time allocated for casting being of necessarily limited duration), they may seem to be fairly conservative in their choices.[12]

It is also the casting director's job to find actors who have been specifically requested for the audition. The casting director needs to be able to track down the phone number of a particular actor's agent (which is usually listed with Equity—so make sure yours is current) or, failing that, a home number (a good reason for an actor without any kind of representation to maintain a *listed* phone number).

The casting director is also responsible for scheduling the audition appointments. He may be a resident casting director on the staff of a theatre company or a gun for hire.

- **The Reader** is a person who has been hired (or forced) to read the sides with the auditioning actors in those instances when actors are not being asked to read with each other. Often, but not always, the reader will be a professional actor. And sometimes you'll find a male reader playing a woman, or vice versa. (If you find yourself reading with a nonactor—say, with an administrative assistant or assistant stage manager—you'll just have to use your imagination and "play through.")

Of Agents and Managers

Although they may not put in an actual appearance at auditions, theatrical agents and managers figure prominently in the audition process.

There is a degree of similarity in what agents and managers do. They both attempt to get jobs for their actor/clients—for a percentage of the clients' income in return, of course. There are

---

12. How many times have I heard a casting director say to a director, "Oh! So you wanna go *that* way . . ."?

three main differences between them. First, a manager will usually take a higher *commission* (percentage of an actor's earnings), usually 15 percent, where an agent will only take 10 percent. The second is a matter of volume: where a manager may have as few as one or two clients or as many as thirty or forty, most agents or agencies have more than sixty. This allows the manager to work more individually and specifically with each client. Which brings us to the third difference—one of philosophy. While an agent is interested almost exclusively in obtaining specific jobs for his clients, a manager is more interested in the long-term career of his clients.

There are, of course, exceptions, so this is not to say that there are *no* agents who are interested in the careers of their clients—after all, the more successful the client, the higher the salary; and the higher the salary, the larger the sum the agent will get in commissions. The fact of the matter is that because a manager has fewer clients, he can devote more time and attention to each individual—and the reason he has fewer clients is so he *can* devote more time and attention to the individual client.

Because we more often hear about managers with actors at the higher end of the success ladder, people wonder whether there is any value for a young, beginning actor to be signed with a manager; after all, they don't have much of a career to be managed. Dan Nani of Nani-Saperstein Management tells me he thinks a manager can be extremely helpful to a neophyte in all aspects of his career: "It's kind of a family relationship. The manager is always there, trying to look out for you and finding ways to help." According to Dan, a good manager can help the beginning actor find a good photographer and help pick successful headshots; he can help in the selection of monologues and songs for auditions, and make sure that the choices are appropriate and valid. Generally he can help the actor be completely prepared for the market by dealing with everything from appropriate dress and makeup to passing along background information about the people the actor will be dealing with. Many agents can also provide help along these lines, but few have the time to do so. And a manager can also help find the right agent for the actor and arrange an introduction and/or audition for him.

Actors who *free-lance* with several agents—that is, work with various agents with whom they do not have an exclusive contract—also find that working with a manager can be helpful in juggling appointments and conflicts. For example, if Agent A wants to submit you for a particular audition, but Agent B has already made the submission, the manager will know this.

However, bear in mind that if you are signed with a manager, and you book a job through an agent's submission, you'll be paying a total 25 percent of your salary to your representation: 10 percent to the agent, 15 percent to the manager.

Go on interviews. Talk with managers *and* agents. Find representation that you feel comfortable with. This will be a business relationship, after all, but it will also be intimate and personal. You want to make sure you have a representative who understands your goals and respects your artistic integrity.

Music Preparation 2

*T*he way your music is presented—its actual physical appearance—can tell a lot about you. A sloppy
audition book gives the impression of sloppy work
habits. Crumpled and torn music can indicate
shabby preparation. And poorly prepared music can lead to
disaster.

As musical director, I attended the callback auditions for
the Goodspeed Opera House production of *Annie 2.*
During the course of the second-to-last day, a fairly well-
known and not untalented cabaret perfomer came in to
sing for the character of Grace, Daddy Warbucks'
unflappable secretary. The extremely large group of us sitting behind the table—in this case, Goodspeed's casting,
artistic, and producing directors; three or four of the
Broadway producers; the production stage manager and
stage manager; Peter Gennaro (the choreographer) and
his assistant, Liza Gennaro; Tom Meehan (the book
writer); Charles Strouse (the composer); Martin Charnin
(the lyricist and director); and myself—began chatting
while this woman discussed her music with the pianist,
Richard Riskin. I noticed that an inordinate amount of
time had passed, which is generally not a good sign—it
either means that the performer doesn't know what she's
doing, the pianist doesn't know what he's doing, or the
music is impenetrable. Having witnessed Richard's
flawless performance during the previous days, I was able
to eliminate him as the cause of the problem.

At last Richard began the introduction, and it was immediately obvious that the actress was uncomfortable about something. She sang about three lines and, as graciously as possible, asked if she could begin again. The introduction began again, this time accompanied by strange glances toward the piano. Once more, about three lines in, she hesitated and stopped. This time the excuses began. "I don't know what the problem is," she said. "It's just not the right feel."

Richard said, "Just tell me what you want."

Again speaking to us, she said, "I usually take along my own pianist, but . . ."

In response, Richard merely held up the music for us to see; it was some hand-drawn lines on a piece of regular loose-leaf paper, with a few scraggly notes and some chord changes.

Still addressing us, the actress said, "I've never had a problem with this music before. All the *good* piano players can deal with it . . ."

At this point, Martin unleashed the temper for which he is famous: "You have no right accusing the pianist for problems created by your inadequately prepared material. We have sat in this room for days and have heard Richard play without error. He is a fine accompanist and your music is *garbage!*" And on and on, each phrase more withering than the previous one. He eventually threw her out of the room, never to be considered again (for this production, anyway).

Most professional audition pianists will attempt to read anything—horrible, hand-scrawled stuff, poorly copied material, bad lead sheets—and will even try to play the music correctly, despite whatever misinformation may appear on the page. But if you are planning to use the pianist who has been hired to play the auditions, you had better take the time and effort to create legible music that is a true representation of what you want and *need* to hear in order to do the best you can.

The Physical Music

Never use your original copy. No matter how careful you may be, there will inevitably come a time when you leave your audition book in the cab or at a restaurant or too close to the edge of the pool or next to the dog's bowl. You will then need to be able to re-create your audition material as quickly as possible. If I had a nickel for every time I've heard some miserable excuse for why an actor has been forced to sing unfamiliar material, I'd be able to buy a boat (a boat?—hmm, another good place to lose your songs).

So, whether your song comes from sheet music, from a photocopy of a book at the library, or from *My Big Book of Successful Audition Songs*, make sure that you are dealing with a copy. Or a copy of a copy. . . .

It is important that the copy be clear and legible. You would be horrified if you had to read a side (a selection of textual material from a show used for auditions) that looked like:

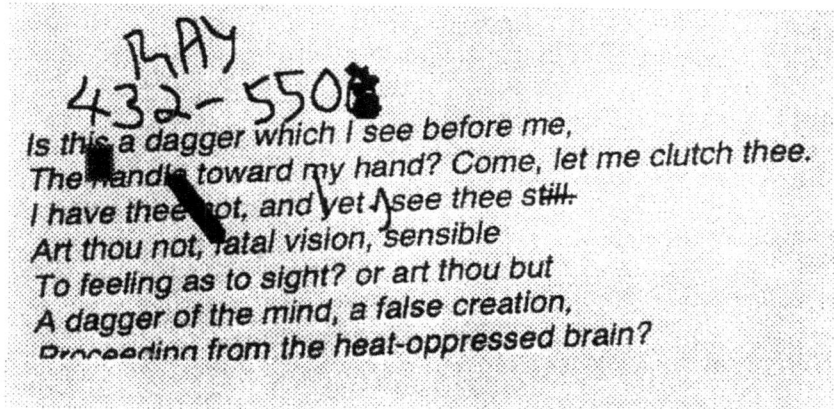

You get the point. Make sure that your original music is as near to perfect as possible. A badly photocopied original will result in bad copies.

Why not try to build a good working relationship with the gang at the copy shop? You'll probably be spending more time there than you'd ever expect, and a little friendliness today could get you one more try on that really nasty original that just won't seem to come out at all.

Your music is going to get dragged around to a zillion auditions and be mistreated by everyone who comes in contact with it. So one of the best things you can do is to make your copies on card stock, a heavy grade of paper (generally between sixty and eighty pounds) that is much more durable than the flimsy twenty-pound stuff you usually copy onto. This will provide you with a strong, long-lasting piece of sheet music. Most larger copy shops carry it in the 8½-inch by 11-inch and 8½-inch by 14-inch sizes; if you'd like to use the larger 11-inch by 17-inch paper (which seems to be the only size that commercially produced music will fit on without reduction), you may have to shop around. Card stock is also stiff enough to support its own weight so that the music doesn't slump over when you place it on edge in the piano rack. It is also less likely to blow away in a draft than the lighter paper.

What do you do if you've brought your music to a copy shop and they've done a bad job? Insist that they do it again! Most places will let you check the first page of a job before they run off the whole thing. So, check your copies. Right away. Don't wait until you're at an audition to discover that the guy at the copy shop inadvertently lopped off the left-hand parts on the bottom of pages two, four, and six. Or that it was copied on such a light setting that the words are illegible and the quarter- and eighth-note heads ($\quarternote$ $\eighthnote$) got hollowed out so that they all look like half notes ($\halfnote$). Look at the copies and compare them to the originals. Is anything missing or cut off? Do you think it could be read in the poor lighting that all rehearsal studios seem to be equipped with? If not, have them do it over!

Now you need a way to keep the sheets of your perfectly copied music together. The best method is to tape the pages side by side. This is how it's done on Broadway and, if you remember from high school band, it's also how it's done with orchestral music. This allows music of fewer than six pages to be spread out flat on most pianos (see Figure 4).

On pianos where stretching the pages out will not work, these taped pages can be accordion-folded into a book. A combination of stretching and folding will also work for more than six pages; the pianist can simply stretch a number of the pages to either side, leaving the center section folded like a book (see Figure 5).

In order for this to work, the music *must* be copied on card stock. Regular-weight paper will create too much of a mess; it will flop over and drip off the sides and fly off the piano if someone walks by.

The neatest way to tape your music together, and one that is used by professional music preparation services, is to place the tape on the *outside* of the fold (see Figure 6).

Properly taped music will usually have the first page facing out when the music is accordioned closed (which will help you identify the piece of music without unfolding it). But before you start taping a song of more than six pages, give some thought to the page turns.

You determine where the page turns fall by whether the first page faces in or out—when page 1 faces out, there will be turns after the odd-page numbers (pages 1, 3, 5, 7, etc.); when page 1 faces in, there will be turns after the even-page numbers (pages

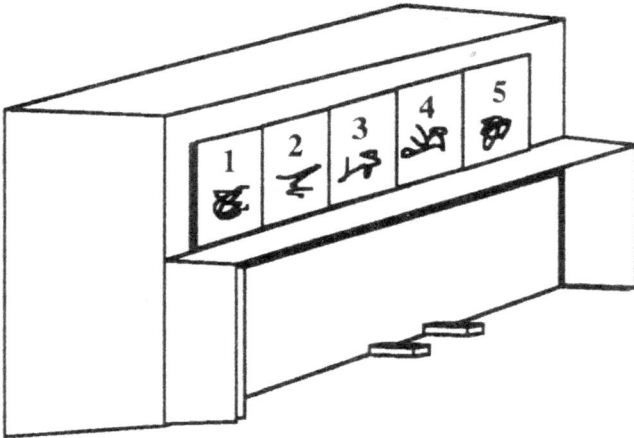

Figure 4

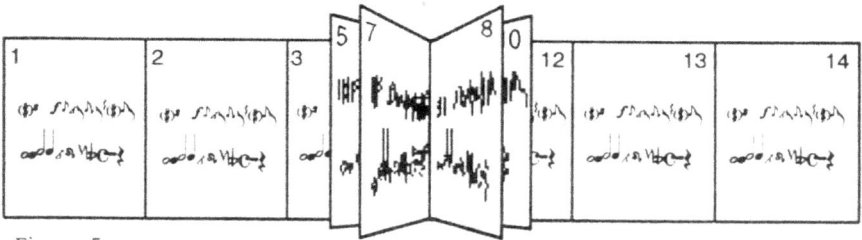

Figure 5

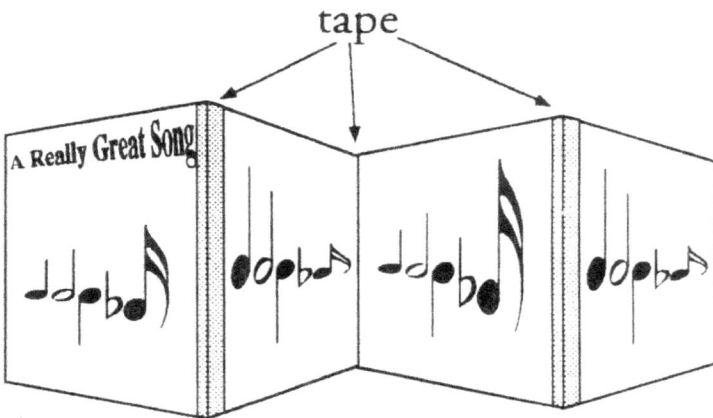

tape

Figure 6

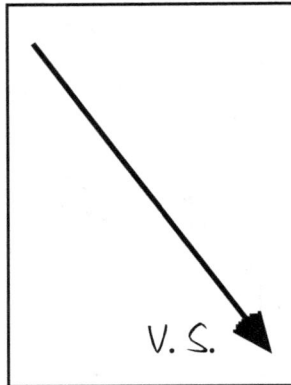

Figure 7*

2, 4, 6, 8, etc.). Remember, every time a pianist's hands have to leave the keyboard in order to turn the page (or for any reason), something is going to be left out of the piano part. Even if you don't read music, some basic logic can help you make decisions about where to put page turns. Do you need to hear a particular chord that would occur on the last few beats before, or the first few beats after, a page turn? Do you need to hear anything consistent in an area that would fall after a page turn? Does a particularly busy-looking piano part fall across a page turn? (Wherever there are *a lot* of notes occurring in a small space—*that's* the busy part.) Puzzle it out, it could help you in the future.

Although it's inadvisable, if it's absolutely necessary to change the turns midway through the piece, in order to keep the remaining page turns as sane as possible, you could insert a blank page marked to show that the music continues after the blank page (see Figure 7).

Use transparent or masking tape. First, place page 1 faceup. Next, place page 2 faceup and to the right of that. Make sure the inside edges are nearly butted together, with about a sixteenth of an inch gap between them. Run a piece of tape nearly the length of the seam. Now flip the music facedown and put page 3 facedown and to the left of page 2. Butt the edges almost together and tape. Flip the music over and put page 4 faceup and to the right of what you have done already. Continue until you're out of pages. If you've decided, for page-turning needs, that page one should face in instead of out, start with step three

* V.S. stands for *Vólti súbito,* meaning "turn the page over quickly."

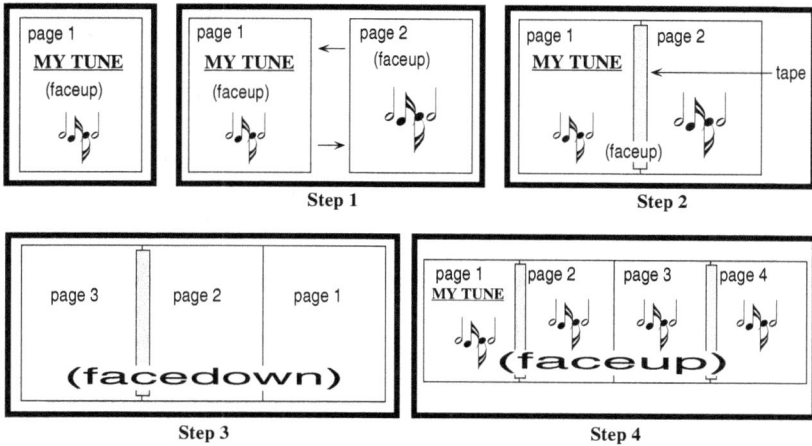

Figure 8

and substitute page 1 for page 2, page 2 for page 3, etc. (see Figure 8).

This will make a nice accordion. Be careful that you don't overlap the sheets or you'll have trouble making a good fold. Also, be careful that you tape in the right order and with the music facing in the right directions. (Sarah once taped all twelve of the pages of "Surabaya, Johnny" in the wrong order—what a mess!)

Many young performers decide to be very organized and use what at first seems to be an excellent, though expensive, method to hold their sheets together: clear plastic loose-leaf page holders. Don't do it. These holders create more problems than they solve. First, a book containing thirty or so audition pieces will be more than 120 pages long, and those plastic things don't come cheap. Second, and more important, they are extremely reflective and trying to read the music through them in the typically poorly lit rehearsal room can be nearly impossible. I cannot begin to describe the gymnastics required, the ducking and dipping, the twisting from side to side, half standing and squatting, all just to try to find a position from which the music is visible.

The best use for these clear plastic holders is for storing complete songs. Once you have taped your music so that it can be folded accordion-style as suggested above, you'll find that you can slip your entire song into a single holder. This makes a nice, neat, compartmentalized audition book—somewhat like a model's portfolio—that you can organize alphabetically by style, by

"The gymnastics required to see through the plastic holders—ducking and dipping, twisting from side to side, half standing, half squatting."

tempo, by whether you want anyone to know you sing that kind of thing, or whatever. The music is held neatly and safely so you won't have the frayed edges and creases you get when you carry loose sheets of music in your knapsack or back pocket.

If, for some strange reason, you are forced to sing a song of inordinate length (if it's only because you *want* to, see the chapter about what to sing), then you can think about (1) using the accordion-fold-with-the-book-in-the-middle-method described above; (2) bringing the original book (if the material was published in book form); or, (3) putting your copied music in a loose-leaf binder. Card stock is not *as* necessary if you plan to use a loose-leaf binder, but it will be more durable in the long run. There is still some preparation involved, however. Don't bring in a book where the music appears only on one side of the page. This means twice as many page turns and page turns are the very thing we want to avoid. Either have your copy made double-sided (back-to-back), or tape the pages together by running a strip of

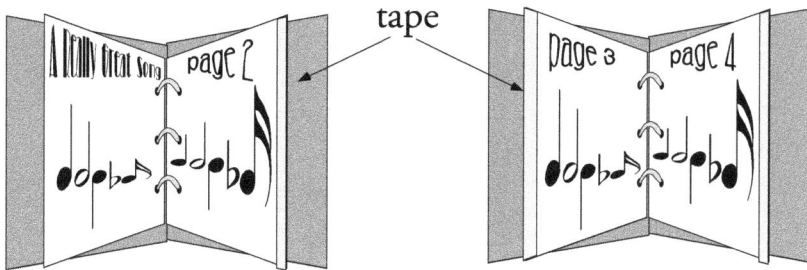

Figure 9

tape along what will be the outside edge (à la step 2 in Figure 8). Be just as careful about where page turns fall as you would with the accordion method (see Figure 9).

Marking Up the Music

I have often been asked if an accompanist finds it insulting to see that a performer has highlighted information in a piece of audition music that would seem fairly obvious to most musicians. My answer is always "Who cares?" The pianist will get over it, and your object is to take every conceivable precaution to guarantee that what you hear is what you *need* to hear in order to do your best. Good pianists know that there are bad pianists out there, and I am not going to take offense if I see that you have circled a key change in three hundred different colors. Calling attention to the obvious can be your best defense against sloppy, or simply sleepy, accompanists.

Therefore *mark everything of importance* (see Figure 10). Buy yourself some highlighters and use them on your carefully prepared music. Not on the original, of course! When you try to photocopy something that has been highlighted, the highlighted area generally appears as a black splotch. At best, the highlighted area will appear as gray, and subsequent highlighting will produce an unreadable, muddy mess on your music. If you're not sure what should be highlighted, ask your accompanist or musical advisor (you've developed this kind of contact by now, right?) to do it for you.

Take care to highlight the following:

- Tempos: initial tempos and tempo changes
- Key signatures: initial key signatures and key changes

A Really Great Song

by Steven M. Alper

Figure 10

- Dynamics
- Repeat signs, multiple endings, codas, and del segni
- Anything else peculiar

Be very careful about borrowing other people's music: if they are as well prepared as you are, their material will be marked up for *their* personal interpretation. This can be confusing for the accompanist and can lead to problems. For instance, even if you have told him to ignore the markings, after a long day of reading carefully marked-up music, it can be difficult for the accompanist to stop reading them.

Transpositions

If you have decided that your music should be performed in a different key from the original, you have several choices. First, you could have the chord changes handwritten above the melody line. I prefer to see the chords in a different color from the music (meaning, usually, anything but black); this greatly aids the eye in finding where to look. You could just circle the chords with a

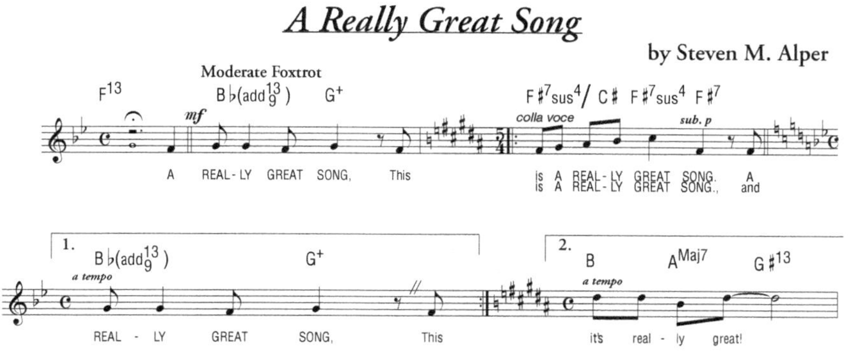
A Really Great Song
by Steven M. Alper
Moderate Foxtrot
mf
colla voce
sub. p
A REAL-LY GREAT SONG, This
is A REAL-LY GREAT SONG. A
is A REAL-LY GREAT SONG., and
a tempo
REAL - LY GREAT SONG, This
it's real - ly great!

Figure 11

color, but that will add a bit of extra visual noise to what is already becoming complicated.

Your second, and slightly better option, would be to have a *lead sheet* prepared. A lead sheet is a piece of music which contains only the melody line with the lyrics and chord symbols (see Figure 11). It may sometimes contain a few instrumental cues for the accompanist at the place where no vocal is occurring (i.e., introductions, modulations, etc.).

If you are having a lead sheet done for you, it should be an accurate depiction of *how you actually do the song*. It should be written in the key in which you sing the song. It should contain, in as linear a form as possible, only the portions of the song you plan to perform; for example, any section that you would not be singing should be omitted, and any bars that are doubled in value should be written out. It should have all the information a full piano/vocal part has (tempos, key signatures, dynamics, repeat signs, and multiple endings), except for the actual piano part. The piano part is basically improvised based on the chord symbols, the rhythm of the melody line, and some descriptions that appear within the lead sheet—in the example above, for instance, notice the smaller (or *cued*) whole note in the first measure and the description, "Moderate Foxtrot."

The chief advantage of the lead sheet over the previous method is that the music will be cleaner and clearer with fewer visual distractions. There will be no extra sets of chord changes to ignore, no superfluous "first endings," and no crossed-out sections.

The final, most valuable option is to have a full piano/vocal part created. This is the fullest representation and would contain everything an accompanist needs to see: all the items appearing in the lead sheet plus a full piano part. It is possible that the *copy-ist (music preparer)* may not feel the need to include chord changes written above the melody, but it is better that these *do* appear (you never know when you'll come up against an accompanist who can *only* read a chord chart). Because the full piano/vocal part is so complete, you are leaving much less to chance, and you will have far fewer surprises since the accompanist is not being required to create an arrangement on the spot (which, of course, you will never have heard before!).

Be aware that the full piano/vocal chart is the most expensive of these options. Nearly all copyists charge by the page, and since the piano/vocal chart contains the most information, it will require the largest number of pages (usually one-and-a-half to three times the number of pages needed for a lead sheet).

Make sure you have someone knowledgeable about music do your transposition for you. The chords printed on sheet music do not always accurately reflect what is going on in the printed piano accompaniment. Here's why: The chord symbols we use nowadays are of fairly recent vintage. Back around the turn of the century, one of the most popular instruments for song accompaniment in the home was, believe it or not, the ukelele. What was needed was a simple and concise method of communicating to a relatively untrained player what the ukelele might play as accompaniment. Part of the solution was the use of a diagram of the fretboard and where and what strings should be depressed (see Figure 12).

In addition to this form of diagram, or *tablature*, a more specific description was needed; a shorter form that would not include the actual tablature. It was decided to use the name of the bottom note of the ukelele chord (what might erroneously be presumed to be the tonic of the chord), plus a symbol or number which would indicate what the upper three notes would be. In other words, the symbol D^7 would indicate that the lowest note of the chord should be a D-natural, the second note up an F-sharp, the third up an A-natural, and the top note a C-natural (see Figure 13).

3rd

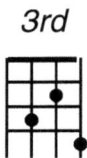

Figure 12

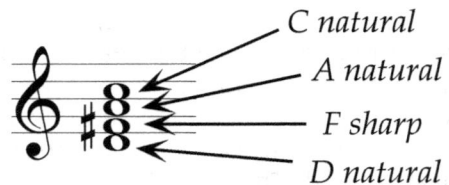

C natural
A natural
F sharp
D natural

Figure 13

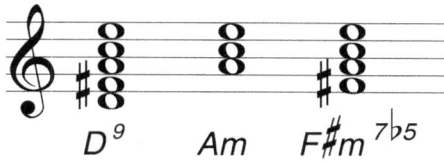

Figure 14

Thus was born our current form of chord symbol notation. Unfortunately for us, however, the four-stringed ukelele was incapable of playing the notes of, say, a five-note chord—a D^9, for instance. Whoever was in charge of making decisions like this would notate only the upper portion of the chord, including just the upper three notes (Am) or four notes ($F\sharp m^{7\flat 5}$ or, in those days, $F\sharp\emptyset$) of the chord (see Figure 14).

Imagine what would happen with a $G\flat 11(\sharp 13\flat 7\flat 5)$:

Things have changed since then. The guitar has risen above the ukelele in stature. Hurray, six strings! Still not enough for the more complex chords. However, the people in a position to label the chords are much more conscientious about things now, but they still tend to make the chords a little simpler when they feel the need. And oftentimes, this will just not cut the mustard. How would you feel, expecting to hear the richness of a D^9 at the peak of your phrase and hearing instead a meager Am? Not terribly happy, I'd bet.

This is why it is important to have someone knowledgeable take on the task of transposing your chord symbols. Unless the music preparer knows what he's doing, you can end up in real trouble.

Finding someone to do your transpositions or music preparation may be a simple thing if your sister or husband is a musician. A *good* musician with a knowledge of harmony and good handwriting can transpose chord changes for you. He may also be able to prepare a lead sheet or piano/vocal chart, but be aware that these require a greater extent of knowledge. And neatness definitely counts. A childish scrawl can lead to an infantile-sounding accompaniment.

If you are not related to any musicians, or don't know one, you can usually find some in your *Yellow Pages* under "Music Preparation Services" or "Music Copyists." Since this is their livelihood, these people are likely to charge more than a friendly musician, but the results will usually be more attractive and more *musical*.

Be wary of people who do music preparation on a computer. Many professionals have been turned off to the potential value of computer-generated music by contact with music preparation dilettantes. The final product can be very beautiful and professional looking, but many computer copyists are not strong musicians. They have been lured into the use of notation software by claims of ease of use and the miraculous conversion of computer-recorded performance into notation. It's not that simple. Music preparation is an art and requires an extensive and sophisticated knowledge of music, both notation and practice.

The costs of music preparation will vary based on your location, the detail required in the music, and whom you find to do it. Although most accompanists or coaches will charge at their hourly rate (anywhere from twenty to sixty dollars per hour) for transposition of the chords on sheet music, I know of one accompanist in New York City who charges only a dollar a page! Lead sheets and piano/vocal parts will run anywhere from six to thirty dollars per page.

Problems

A point that cannot be emphasized strongly enough is this: Make sure you try out your new arrangements *before* they are used at an audition. I have often heard the excuse, after particularly unsuccessful auditions, "Well, I never heard the accompaniment before." This is one of the lamest, most tired alibis in use and generally evokes little sympathy. It is considered poor preparation, almost in the same league as asking if it would be all right to hold the book for your monologue while you perform it.

If your regular accompanist is the same person who does your music preparation, see if you can rope someone else into just reading the new chart through to spot any errors in notation. Failing this, make sure you run through the arrangement several times; repetition tends to point up problems. (I can't tell you how many times I've played a supposedly error-free work before uncovering a simple mistake that I had been correcting with my ear.)

Something else I hear often: "There's always a problem when we get to that spot. I don't know why." If you find, after performing a piece at several auditions, that a problem consistently occurs at a certain point in the music, *find out what is causing the problem and get it fixed!* It could be caused by a mistake in the piano part or by some inaccurate or confusing notation. There is the possibility that the section contains some degree of difficulty that is causing the accompanists to choke, in which case you should either bring your own player to the audition, or have the problem spot reworked to simplify it.

Properly prepared and notated music will be read and played effectively by a competent accompanist—and, as a matter of fact, will probably give him a great deal of pleasure (which you only stand to benefit from). Providing the accompanist with all the information he needs to do his job well will make it possible for him to give you the best support he can, so you can give the best audition you can.

The Care and 3
Feeding of the
Piano Player

Treat Him Well

*A*ccompanying a singer is a specialized art. Just because a pianist is an excellent player does not necessarily mean he will be a sympathetic accompanist. Besides the basic playing skills, an accompanist needs to have the ability to comprehend and react to nearly subliminal cues presented by a singer. For example, is the amount of time between a singer's breath and her next sung note a subconscious indication of a new tempo? Or is the singer trying to create a ritard (a slowing down of the tempo) or merely back-phrasing (deliberately singing "behind the beat")? The ability to make such subtle distinctions on the fly can only come from the experience of playing for many different singers.

An accompanist is expected to be familiar with the entire range of musical theatre styles as well as to have a fairly extensive knowledge of the widest range of audition material. (Sometimes an accompanist is hired based on his specialties—i.e., opera/operetta, jazz, rock.) He is expected to be an excellent musician capable of playing the most difficult music from the standard repertoire, able to sight-read fluently, and able to read and interpret lead sheets and chord charts. He should be experienced at accompanying singers, able to follow accurately and to anticipate the needs and intentions of the performer. He should, at the very *least*, be able to play the music from the show you are auditioning for.

My Buddy

As a beginning auditioner, you may be unaware that the accompanist provided at an audition is one of your greatest assets. You have to consider him your dearest friend in the room. He *is* there to support you and to provide the platform from which you will achieve success.

However, you would do well to realize that just as he is able to *support* you, he is also able to wreak havoc on your audition. There are a million subtle and nearly undetectable ways in which an accompanist can deliberately screw you up if he decides that he doesn't like you. He can, for example, insidiously vary the tempos to keep you constantly off balance. Or he can simply fail to be there to help you if, for some reason, you make a mistake. Most active, working accompanists are highly moral and professional and would consider (as I do) the practice of any act of sabotage unethical and downright evil. Still, you never know. . . .

How to Handle a Pianist

Therefore it is always in your best interest to treat the accompanist cordially and with respect, regardless of his competency.

Greet the accompanist as you would anyone in a business situation. If you know his name, use it; eventually, you'll get to know most of your local accompanists (and be able to anticipate problems if you can learn who is playing in advance of your audition).

Think twice about shaking hands. *I* don't have a problem with it, but Mary Sugar, a New York City accompanist, tells me that since she greets quite a few actors in the course of an average day of auditions, her hands begin to swell and become painful from all the hand-wringing. If you do feel a handshake is in order, don't feel the need to impress the accompanist with your strength!

Be professional and courteous about your needs. Point out the important aspects of your music:

- Find out from your rehearsal accompanist or coach exactly what these are. If you are not a musician, it is quite possible that you will waste time overstating the obvious. Since your music has (of course) been properly marked, it is fine to say, "I have highlighted all the key and meter changes as well as the tempo changes." Pointing out fermatas (those little bird's-eye-looking-things that mean hold indefinitely), accelerandi, repeat signs, and the like, even though they have been highlighted, is good practice. You will especially want to call attention to anything that places extra demands on the accompanist, such as rubato or exceptionally free sections, or anything peculiar (i.e., "I back-phrase the entire song; just keep playing in tempo, please.").
- Indicate the tempos of each section of your song. This is very important. Many times people have simply handed me their music and walked away. Even if you are performing a very well-known piece of music, do not assume that you and the accompanist agree on what the standard tempo is (the first three arrangements I did of "N.Y.C." from *Annie* were as ballads). When describing tempos, do not snap your fingers or stamp your foot. The best and most direct way to communicate a tempo is to quietly sing the first few measures of the song or section. Remember that I said, "quietly." This is between you and the accompanist. You don't want to give away your whole act before you even get started, do you?
- Most accompanists (as well as the people behind the table) expect you to take a moment before you begin. Sarah tells me that one should not take this for granted; she has encountered accompanists who suddenly begin playing for no apparent reason. Just to be on the safe side, ask the pianist to watch for your nod and (hopefully) he will wait for the cue from you to begin.

No matter what has occurred during your audition, when you have finished singing or when you are leaving the room, be sure to thank the pianist. This is not only a matter of politeness; it gives the impression that you are in control of the situation by acknowledging the fact that, while you were in the room, the accompanist was essentially working for you.

Try not to ask more of a pianist than is humanly possible. Do not bring illegible or ambiguous music or music that requires a greater amount of time to explain than to perform. Do not bring anything that is overly complicated to sight-read or too difficult to play. *Do* follow the guidelines presented in Chapter 2, "Music Preparation."

The Great Unknown

Even though he is apparently a mere accompanist, or even if he has been introduced as the accompanist, you cannot tell for sure exactly who he is (or will be in the future) or what position he holds (or will hold).

I was called in to interview for the position of musical director for the original production of Randy Courts' and Mark St. Germain's *The Gifts of the Magi*. As will sometimes occur, I received a call shortly thereafter informing me that the job had gone to someone else.

Prior to my scheduled interview, I had agreed to play for the auditions—a situation which now seemed a little awkward, but which I planned to deal with as best I could.

At the end of the first day of auditions, Carolyn Rossi-Copeland, the producer, asked me if I would take a walk with her so that she could have a little chat with me. It seems that the creators were having some trouble with the originally hired musical director (a gentleman with whom I have subsequently become good friends), who had opinions and ideas about the piece that were in conflict with their own. I was asked if *I* would be interested in taking over the position.

So, on the second day of auditions, I was now the musical director. Imagine the surprise of those actors at the callbacks—who had shamelessly schmoozed the former musical director and had looked down their noses at the poor lowly accompanist—when they saw who was in charge now! *[diabolical laughter.]*

He could be the musical director/conductor of the show and might have every bit as much to say as the director or the choreographer about whether or not you get cast. He could be a very close friend of someone on the production team. (You wouldn't want something deleterious about you to come out during a date between this accompanist and the producer or even immediately after you leave the room.)

Just because he is only a lowly accompanist for this audition doesn't mean he won't appear in a position of power the next time you encounter him. He could turn out to be the conductor, composer, director, or who knows, the choreographer. He probably *is* a composer anyway (who isn't?); many successful musical theatre composers have been known to play for auditions. (I've been told that, because of his love of accompanying, Charles Strouse continued to work as an accompanist even after the success of his musical, *Bye, Bye Birdie.*)

Even if he is "just" an accompanist, you should still treat him courteously and with respect. You are a professional, after all. Besides, the musical theatre community is fairly insular, and you don't want *anyone* bad-mouthing you.

Following her audition for *Up Against It* at the New York Shakespeare Festival, a young woman stormed out of the room ranting, "That little shit. That horrible awful man. I hate him." Sarah, who was waiting to audition for the show herself, asked who had upset her.

"That musical director. He hates me! If I had known it was him, I wouldn't have bothered to audition."

Sarah revealed that the "little shit" was her husband, in other words—*me.*

The woman was mortified; the blood drained from her face. She tried to apologize. Sarah explained that I was not without problems (*thanks,* Sarah), but, she wondered, what could I have possibly done to upset her so much?

The woman said that she had been involved in a production with me before and it had become obvious to her then that I didn't like her work and that I wished that she hadn't been hired.

When I got home that evening, Sarah told me what had happened. It was my turn to be mortified. The woman had given an excellent audition, and, in fact, her resume photo was still sitting in the "possible callback" pile. I called her immediately to try to clear things up.

The production we had worked on together was part of the New York University Musical Theatre Program, a program for lyricists and composers which culminates in a four-day professional workshop. The particular piece we had worked on contained some incredibly complicated and dense music. The time that we had was completely insufficient to learn the material. And the reason this woman thought I disliked her was this: I was so concerned with the work that needed attention that I neglected what was working. This woman knew her material and was doing an excellent job. Her performance was wonderful. So I had nothing to do with her! I was too busy dealing with the three guys who couldn't carry a tune and had to sing in three-part, contrapuntal harmony. I made the mistake of not letting her know how well she was doing.

I've since learned to bestow praise in addition to criticism (something, by the way, not everyone in the business has

learned). And she may have learned to be a little more circum-
spect.

Why Does He Do the Things He Does?

It is a mistake to assume that the people behind the table are
unaware of the problems presented by an inept accompanist. In
a truly professional situation it is possible that the auditors have
found themselves stuck with an accompanist they are unhappy
with. They may have already lined up a replacement. (I've been
called at 10:15 A.M. asking me to get to an audition session that
began at 10:00, as soon as possible, to take over for someone
who is not working out.)

The way you handle yourself in the face of inept accompaniment can show you in a positive light. Your poise and continued
control of the situation can be seen as a reflection of the way you
would handle yourself in a "live" theatre situation. If you behave
as if everyone is aware of the pianist's failings and refuse to call
attention to the problems he has created, you will seem to have
risen above the hazards you have been presented.

Arggggh . . .

I don't mean to scare you so much as prepare you for the
inescapable worst. One day you will walk into an audition, after
having meticulously prepared yourself for every aspect of the
audition (as always), only to discover that the accompanist is not
capable of providing you with the support you expect.

Dealing with a problem accompanist is practically an art form
in itself. Basically, you will have to continue to barrel through in
spite of any disaster which may occur. Here are some specific problems you might face, and suggestions for how to handle them.

1. The accompanist has never before been involved with (or
   possibly even dislikes) the theatre.
   What to do: Don't panic; you may not be in a problem situation. Properly communicating your needs will allow a good
   player to accompany your performance of "I Cain't Say No"
   (from *Oklahoma*) as well or nearly as well as a seasoned theatrical accompanist.

2. The accompanist tells you he can't play your song because he has never heard of it.

   What to do: Choose another song. Be aware, however, that it rarely matters if the pianist knows the song you are handing him. A good accompanist will be able to play your song whether or not he has heard it or played it before—providing (of course!) that your music has been adequately and accurately notated, modified, and marked. The exception is when the music is *so* complicated (tempo changes, feel and/or style changes, or difficulty of accompaniment) that you might have considered bringing your own accompanist in the first place. With this type of difficult material, it would be in your best interest to find out if the pianist has a knowledge of the piece before deciding whether or not to go ahead with it. Through your experience of having tested your audition material on accompanists of varying abilities, you will eventually learn what material can or cannot be sight-read by an adequate accompanist.

3. The accompanist is reputed to play a mean boogie-woogie but cannot seem to do justice to the Handel aria you brought (or vice versa).

   What to do: Make the most of it. Play through. It's possible to find that a boogie-woogie-influenced accompaniment to your classical aria can lead you to discover a positive new interpretation you would not have been able to find in a more traditional way.

4. The accompanist slows the tempo down whenever you arrive at the more difficult sections because he is having trouble with the playing.

   What to do: You have no choice but to go with him. Running on ahead without him will not only cause a mess, it will also be obvious that you are straying from the accompaniment. Although *we* know it is not your fault, not tracking along with what is going on around you will make you appear oblivious. Be aware that a different tempo is going to present you with deviations from your preset choices. For example, a much slower tempo will probably require more frequent breaths than your regular tempo does.

5. The accompanist tells you he can only read a full piano part, not lead sheets.

   What to do: Choose another song which *does* have a full piano part. (You should have brought an accompaniment that contained both.)

6. The accompanist tells you he can only read lead sheets, not a full piano part.

   What to do: This is a very rare occurrence, and whoever has done the hiring has made a drastic error. Choose another song which has the chord changes written or printed above. (If you had been made aware of the accompanist problem before you arrived, you undoubtedly would have brought an accompaniment that contained both chord changes and full accompaniment—with the chord changes above the melody line—or your own accompanist.)

7. The accompanist ignores you. He plays at a tempo different from the one you initially provided. He doesn't follow when you speed up, or he slows down when you get faster, or he gets loud when you get quiet.

   What to do: You will have to go along with the accompaniment. Try to have a good time with it. Make new discoveries. If it's not working at all, stop the song gracefully and, also gracefully, ask permission to do something else.

8. The theatre company has not provided the accompanist with the music or the song from the show you are auditioning for.

   What to do: Be happy because you brought your own copy of the music.

Jack, a friend of mine, having appeared in the role of Pseudolus in several productions of *A Funny Thing Happened on the Way to the Forum* at highly esteemed regional theatres—including a production which had concluded less than a month before—was called in to audition for the same role at yet another regional theatre. After a thorough preparation, he went to the audition having made the not unreasonable assumption that the theatre company would have the score for the show on hand. He strode into the room with his usual ebullient confidence. The accompanist immediately informed him that they did not, in fact, have a copy of the score. Jack then realized that, although he had brought a copy of "Free" (the song he had intended to sing from the show), it had been extensively edited to be of the shortest possible length. (The only time he would consider doing the full version is when auditioning for the role. Like now.)

Things started to look a little brighter once he had spent a minute with the accompanist figuring out how to expand the song to some degree, but once the song began, Jack discovered to his horror that the music was beyond the player's ability to sight-read.

To hear Jack tell it, the performance was nearly too excruciating to endure and not at all the success he had anticipated.

There is an almost-happy ending to this story, however. Because the audition was held well in advance of the production, Jack was asked to come back and reaudition about a month later. At which time the theatre did think to provide a copy of the score. So did Jack.

9. The accompanist has a terribly obnoxious, annoying, and overbearing attitude and is destroying your concentration and poise.
   What to do: Be twice as nice. Maintain your concentration. Don't take it personally. The guy obviously has some kind of problem and being too sensitive will make your audition a waste of time. Hopefully, he plays so well that his attitude won't matter.

Finally, if playing the piano seems to be a brand-new experience for the accompanist, just do the best you can. Everyone else who is auditioning will have had to deal with the same pianist, and you can still follow through with your objective of being the best and most appropriate performer for the role despite the incompetent accompaniment.

Bringing Your Own

When I am asked on what occasions an actor should bring his own accompanist to an audition, I answer "always." Why not; you've been rehearsing with your own accompanist, so you know he can play the material and you know you'll be comfortable with him. The reason you don't, of course, is the expense. Paying someone somewhere between thirty and seventy dollars a few times a week can get prohibitively expensive fast! You could do what Sarah did (marry your accompanist), but if that doesn't seem feasible, just hire an accompanist for special auditions (e.g., your first Broadway audition) so that you'll be more at ease. Bring him when you have specially prepared material, something you've worked up that requires a rehearsed accompanist. You should bring him when you know that the material you'll be singing is too difficult to be sight-read by the average audition accompanist. Finally and definitely, bring him if, by doing some advance research, you have found out that the house accompanist is a known incompetent.

And, no, people don't mind if you bring your own. They're not insulted—and the resident accompanist can usually use the break!

"I can't read music. Just start singing and I'll join in."

The Song 4

Of all the elements that make up a good musical theatre audition, the selection of song material is, on the whole, the most important. Your audition material should be like an ideal outfit of clothing: fitting perfectly, highlighting your strengths, and disguising (or avoiding) your weaknesses.

What to Sing

When the time comes to make the decision about what to sing at your audition, you need to consider above all the primary goals of your audition: (1) to show yourself to your best advantage and (2) to convince the casting panel that you are right for the job.

Showing yourself off should not be a hard thing for you to do—it's probably the reason you got involved with this business in the first place. The desire to sing and/or dance and/or act, to appear in front of an audience to one extent or another, is common to performers. The problem is in showing yourself off *well*, in finding material that shows you in your best light. Many young performers simply choose songs they like or just happen to know, and these may not be the most effective sales tools. I'm not saying that you shouldn't like your material, just that these particular selections may not be best suited for the task at hand.

Bearing in mind the idea of showing yourself off well, the songs you choose should allow you to display

1. your talents as a singer.
2. your abilities as a musician.
3. your skills as an actor.
4. your ability to carry a role.

Let's take a deeper look at how a song can lend to an artful display of your talents.

1. **Showing off your talents as a singer.** You want your material to allow you to demonstrate your singing strengths and skills. Do you have a particularly high belt or a good, strong mix?[13] Are you particularly skilled at rapid passages? Can you do pop or country or true legit?[14] Are you a low bass? A baritone? A tenor? A very high tenor? Or a low alto? A high soprano? (Your song choices should always be within your range.)

2. **Demonstrating your abilities as a musician.** Your material should allow you to show that you have a good sense of rhythm, can keep a beat, and can stay on pitch. (You can think

---

13. The term *belting* is used to describe a kind of "oversinging," usually by a woman. Technically speaking, what is occurring on a basic level is that breath is pushed through the vocal folds, forcing a faster than normal vibration for the range. Its use is strictly contemporary.

Mixing is applicable to both women and men and is commonly used to describe a blending of the chest and head voices to extend the range of the chest voice into a higher register and create a stronger tone than the straight use of head voice would permit.

Author's Tirade: I suggest that, rather than singing to these labels, the singer concern herself with creating a consistent tone across the entire range: an easing of the lower range into the upper range and a matching of the extremes. A good teacher avoids the use of such labels. However, this is a kind of touchy subject. No matter what your vocal quality is, no matter how you've been taught to produce sound, you are going to have to deal with these labels. Let's say that you *have* learned to produce a continuous and consistent tone throughout your range. Inevitably, the day will come when you are asked to belt. You will have to give some sort of imitation of the belting sound, something which will be contrary to what you have been taught. It's an unfortunate and inescapable evil. People in power have different likes and dislikes, and sadly, some people in charge are not necessarily the most educated in the area of vocal production.

14. The term *legit* refers to nonpop singing, not contemporary. A focused sound. More traditional and much closer in style and physical production to opera than to rock.

of this as an extension to "Showing off your talents as a singer.")

3. **Using your skills as an actor.** In the theatre, a successful song will have some sort of point of view. You won't find many songs about *nothing* (and if you do, you probably won't remember them). A theatrically successful song will contain emotion and/or insight into the character who is singing. There will be something to act, some meat for the performer to chew on.

   As much as any monologue, your song should have something for the actor in you to do, a character for you to play, emotions to sing about. (This is why strong actors who can barely sing are often cast in musicals: they have the ability to *act* the role.)

4. **Showing off your ability to carry a role.** Your song choices should allow you to be in control *all of the time.* You should be the one creating the impulses that drive the song forward. The character you are actively creating is coming up with the lyrics you are singing. Motion and emotion keep moving throughout the performance of the song. (You can think of this as an extension to "Using your skills as an actor.")

Researching the Role

It is equally important for you to prove that you are not only talented in all performance areas, but that your talents also make you the best and only conceivable choice for the role you're up for. Being a brilliant talent doesn't count for much if your talents are inappropriate for what the casting people are looking for. You have the difficult task of showing off how you are both qualified for the job and suitable for the role.

In order to make an appropriate selection of material, you will have to do some research about the role you are auditioning for. Here are the four most important questions to answer.

1. **What is the style of the show?** Is it a comedy? Serious? A farce? Straight? Tongue-in-cheek? A parody? A play with music as opposed to a musical? A traditional linear musical? A revue? (Generally speaking, in the revue form, character development is rarely important—we are usually presented with personalities rather than created characters. Performers are usually cast either for their real-life personas or for their ability to switch quickly between characters.)

2. **Who is the character?** What's the character's name? Who is the character and what kind of role is it? Comedic? Dramatic? Angry? Mean? Ditsy? Flighty? Studious? Narrow-minded? Old? Young? Sexy? Religious? Terminally ill? A waitress? A truck driver? An astrophysicist?

3. **What is the vocal range of the role?** What notes will the performer of the role be expected to sing? And with what kind of tone or style? Are they, for example, looking for a soprano? An alto? A soprano who belts? A tenor? An extraordinarily high tenor?

   (Many times in new shows the range of a role will be open to change based on who is finally cast. The creative team will move keys around and/or rewrite sections and whole songs to fit the strengths of the actor who has been given the part. This is less often the case in revivals or regional productions and is pretty rare in stock productions where time is limited.)

4. **What kind of song(s) does the character sing?** A torch song? A patter song? Heavy metal? Bluegrass? Bel canto? Rodgers-and-Hart-style traditional musical comedy?

How do you find the answers to these questions? If you are responding to a casting notice in a trade paper (e.g., *Backstage, Hollywood Reporter*), the published *breakdown* will usually give you most of the information you need.

You'll most often see something like this:

BELCH, BOOT, AND CANDIES
10 am–8 pm, Jan. 24 and 25 at
10th Avenue Studios, 3174 3rd Ave., 4th Fl.
THE IRONIC ACTIVITY THEATRE of Cleveland, PA (casting dir.: Gertrude Gecco) is casting for a production of **BELCH, BOOT, AND CANDIES** (by **Winken, Blinken and Nod**; dir.: **Hans Zoff**; chor.: **Beenie N. Cecille**; mus. dir.: **TBA**). Seeking singing actors for the following roles: **BELCH**, late-40's–early-50's, low bass (must have low D!), angry but earnest taxicab driver of eastern European descent. **BOOT**, mid-20's, high-belt (to an E), a sexy vamp (a la a young Marlene Dietrich), strong, but with a heart of gold. **THE CANDY TWINS**: **JOSEF**, ingenue male, tenor, extremely handsome and muscular, extremely stupid; **JOSEFINA**, ingenue, soprano, pretty body builder, extremely bright. For all roles, prepare an up-tempo and a ballad in a traditional musical comedy style (Rodgers and Hart).
Accompanist provided.

A listing like this gives you everything you need to know. If, for instance, you decide that the role of "Josefina" is right for you, you can see that you need to prepare

1. An up-tempo and a ballad;
2. In traditional musical comedy style;
3. Neither of which should sound "belted" (only soprano);
4. Which somehow demonstrates that the character is intelligent; and
5. You should wear something that makes you look a little "pumped up."

When a show is ready to go into casting, the casting director will often distribute to theatrical agents and managers a listing very similar to the one you would see in the trade papers. The agents and managers then review these character breakdowns and send in pictures and resumes (or just call in the names) of their clients (and freelancers) who they think are appropriate to the roles.

If you have been submitted by an agent or have been contacted directly by a casting agent, either should be able to provide you with the breakdown information. If for some reason they don't volunteer this information, make sure you ask. Don't go into an audition cold, without any knowledge of the character you are up for.

In many cases, you'll be able to find out a lot on your own. If this is a regional or stock production or a revival of an established show, you can often find scores, scripts, and recordings in your local library or at your sheet music dealer. You may even have friends who have copies of stuff. You can learn a lot more about a character from a script, or about the musical style of a piece from a score or recording than you can from what your agent reads you from a breakdown. A breakdown might say: "**Nellie Forbush**, 20s/30s, good belt, nurse, perky and not as tough as she thinks she is."[15] But of course there's a lot more to her than that.

Study whatever materials you can get your hands on. The more familiar you are with the piece, the better prepared you'll be for your audition.

If you don't read music and haven't found a recording of the

---

15. Nellie Forbush is from *South Pacific,* by Rodgers, Hammerstein, and Logan.

show, but you've found some sheet music or the score, find someone to play through some selections. You'll be able to get a sense of the show's style from a few numbers.

I am often asked whether it is obligatory to sing a song from the show you are auditioning for. There's no easy answer to this one. If you are asked to sing a song from the show, then you'd better. If it's been left open, and you don't already have a song from the show in your repertoire, you may not have the time to learn something new. If you already know a piece from the show, but feel more prepared to do something that's similar instead, I suggest you spend a little time refamiliarizing yourself with the piece from the show and have it with you in case the audition panel decides that they *need* to hear you sing something from the show. But remember, you're always better off telling them you don't know anything from the show than botching a poorly pre-pared selection. Offer something appropriate, something stylisti-cally similar instead.

(In my more than twenty years in the business, only once have I heard of people casting a show and telling actors specifically *not* to sing something from the show. I'm sure they had their reasons, but I can't fathom what they might have been.)

More About Appropriateness

If, for some reason, you can't pull together an audition piece that's appropriate for the character you'll be auditioning for, at least try to find something that's stylistically appropriate for the show. Pick something that *could* be sung by a character in the show. Or something that could be sung by a character in a differ-ent show by the same composer.

If you're called to audition for a brand-spanking-new show for which there are no scripts, sides, or scores available, see what you can find out about the writers of the piece. Especially the composer. Survey a range of material—if the composer has been around for a while, looking at a single show won't do the trick. Her style is bound to change to suit each show and to have at least undergone some kind of change over the years. For exam-ple, if you were to have been asked to audition for *Rags,* with Charles Strouse's music, listening to *Annie* wouldn't have been too helpful to your preparation.

Sometimes just the process of digging around can be helpful in itself. Gems may be revealed, not just for research for this particular audition, but for helping you to uncover new audition material as well. Did you know that Charles Strouse wrote an opera for children called *The Nightingale*? It contains some fabulous music. And listening to *The Nightingale* would have been more helpful in preparing for your theoretical *Rags* audition than listening to *Annie* would have been, since the score of *The Nightingale* is stylistically closer to *Rags*. (The difference is *so* vast it is almost hard to recognize it as the work of the same composer.)

Sometimes, by the way, when you're auditioning for a new show, you'll be handed a piece of sheet music and asked to prepare it for your audition. It's possible that you'll be provided with some kind of demo recording to help you learn it, but more than likely you'll be left on your own. In this case, if you can't play it yourself, you'll have to find someone to play it for you. And if, while working with your accompanist or coach, you discover that the key has to be changed in order to do justice to the song and to yourself, you'll have to make the necessary transposition. In this case, you probably should plan on bringing your accompanist to the audition with you, because you can't expect the provided accompanist to do the transposition for you. And don't be surprised if you are asked to sing the song in the original key in spite of your objections. The authors may feel a particular attachment to the original key (maybe because it's part of a duet, has a particular key relationship to another song, etc.).

Elizabeth Howell (who appeared as the Mother Superior in the original production of *The Sound of Music* and who is a voice teacher I have always enthusiastically recommended) tells a story about auditioning for the original production of *The Yearling*. While working on the piece they had given her to learn, she realized that she just could not do a good job with the song in the key it was written in. She figured out what key would work better for her and wrote it down on the top of the music.

Now, you'd think for a *Broadway* audition that this would not have been a problem, but when she got there, nobody in the room was capable of playing the song in the transposed key! And poor Elizabeth had to struggle through it in the original key.

Another question I am often asked is whether to sing a song by the composer of the work you are auditioning for if the composer is in the room. This is rarely a mistake. What could be more appropriate? (Most composers enjoy hearing their work!) Bear in mind, however, that few people are as familiar with the material as the composer is, and you'll be judged based on her knowledge of the way the piece can be and has been performed. Also, unless you are very aware of the composer's intentions, be careful about deviating from the printed score. You'll be dead in the water if the composer feels you have done an injustice to her work.

Whatever you sing, at least learn the basic information about it. Know the names of the composer, the lyricist, and what show the song is from. And you had better at least know the title—the correct title! For instance, the song from *Oklahoma* is called "People Will Say We're in Love," not "Don't Throw Bouquets at Me." It will reflect badly on you if you're asked about your song and you can't come up with the answers.

During an arduous set of non-Equity auditions one muscle-bound Brooklyn-born actor could not seem to get things right. Aside from peculiarities of diction ("There's a pla-*YEECE* for us."), he couldn't come up with the right information about his song. He came into the room and announced "I'm gonna sing 'Wha Snoo?' by Linda Ronstadt." ("What's New?" by Johnny Burke and Bob Haggart had appeared on a recent Linda Ronstadt album.) He then introduced his next selection by saying, "I'm gonna be singin' 'Deh's A Pla-*YEECE* For Us,' by Bahbruh Streisan." ("Somewhere" from *West Side Story,* lyrics by Stephen Sondheim, music by Leonard Bernstein, had recently appeared on Barbra Streisand's *Broadway* album.) And even after seeing our shock and annoyance, this gentleman stood firm in his belief that these songs had been written by Ronstadt and Streisand!

Special Arrangements

Should you do specially prepared arrangements of songs? This will usually be ruled out when you are singing a song from the show you're auditioning for. It's inadvisable to walk into auditions for *Fiddler on the Roof* with your really cool cabaret arrangement of "Anatevka." (I can't say that this is *always* the wrong thing to do, but it's the kind of choice that can only be made with experience and knowledge of the people you're auditioning for.)

I was in Cy Coleman's office playing the auditions for *Let 'Em Rot* (which later moved on to Broadway as *Welcome to the Club*). I was much younger and working for such an important person made me more than a little uncomfortable. I was pretty jittery just doing the regular stuff, reading people's music, doing an occasional sight transposition, etc., when a guy came in, handed me his music—"Real Live Girl," from *Little Me* (by Carolyn Leigh and *Cy Coleman!*)—and asked me not just to sight-transpose it, but also to change the arrangement of the song from a waltz to a fast

polka, there on the spot. I nearly exploded in a fit of projectile per-
spiration. How could this guy take this kind of chance?—not only
distorting the work of the composer to his very face, but also
putting this kind of pressure on me! (Because the results are so
unpredictable, this is exactly the kind of thing I've been telling
you *never* to do.)

Despite the obstacle presented by my excessive shpritzing,
we managed to get through it rather well and when it was all
over I looked up to see Mr. Coleman grinning with amusement.
He really seemed to get a kick out of this choice. But what I
didn't find out until after the number was over is that he had
worked with this actor many times before, so there was much
less risk involved than I had thought.

(The man didn't get cast, but because he wasn't right for the
role, not because of his choice.)

A great arrangement is one of the best ways to show yourself
off, especially if it's been created specifically for you. However, I
feel that paying for a new arrangement to use only for auditions
is an unjustifiable expense. I suggest that you acquire a new special arrangement only when:

1. It occurs conveniently. You've just finished working in a
   revue, and you've gotten permission to use that rousing
   arrangement that knocked 'em dead every night.
2. You regularly work with a coach, and part of the process is
   providing you with new arrangements tailored to your skills.
3. You have an idea *so* inspired it just *has* to be done.

Even making simple modifications to a piece of music can be
considered "arranging" it. Having a song written out because of a
transposition, adding a modulation, trimming a few extraneous
repetitions or piano solos, or changing the last few bars of the
ending from blah to sock-o is actually making the most basic of
arrangements.

By the way, you don't *need* to have the grooviest arrangements to get work: I know an older actor who works all the time,
and at every audition he plunks down the same ragged, dog-eared
copy of "The Most Beautiful Girl in the World" (from the musical
extravaganza, *Jumbo*) that he's been using for forty years!

If It Ain't on the Page . . .

If you often work with the same accompanist, especially one
who plays for your auditions, songs that you perform with some

regularity will have a tendency to develop into arrangements over time and without anything getting written out. I often go with Sarah to play two of her main audition pieces. We've been doing them for years. For one of them, I play a rather wild improvisation based on the sheet music. For the longest time, the other wasn't written out at all—it was just in my head! But what do you think happened the first time I wasn't available to play for her? For a big callback?! No music. . . . I had to stay up all night preparing *something* for an accompanist to read. (But she still makes me go and play them for her. She says no one plays them as well as I do—shameless flatterer!)

A few years back I was hired to help put together a little off-Broadway revue with music of the 1950s that was scheduled to run in a small club downtown. After several days of auditioning, a young woman came in with her accompanist. We watched with no small degree of confusion as she led him by the hand up to the stage. Once up on the stage, she introduced herself and the accompanist—who seemed to be staring dazedly into an empty area of the club. It wasn't until one of us spoke and he focused in our direction that we realized he was blind. Then we watched as he scooted the piano bench nearly off the back of the stage. The stage manager leapt up and, grabbing the back of the bench, told the startled pianist about the limited area he had to work with.

The audition then proceeded: the woman was an excellent performer with a lovely voice and we listed her for a callback. She left the room, once again leading her accompanist by the hand.

When the callbacks were held a week later, I was serving as accompanist. We were all suffering from that kind of general torpor one gets after an extended period of auditioning—listlessness, the inability to focus for any extended period, and the feeling that we had inadvertently scheduled the callbacks from the reject pile. And so we were very happy to hear the monitor announce that this young woman would be next. Assuming that she would be bringing her accompanist along, I left the piano and sat down with the rest of the auditors. She came in and marched up to the stage. Alone. She explained that her accompanist was ill. And then burst into tears. She said that she couldn't provide the music for her songs *because her accompanist was blind and never used any music!*

It all worked out fine in the end. She and I put our heads together and came up with a couple of songs that she knew and I could fake. After all, these were 1950s, three-chord, Rock and Roll tunes we're talking about.

So what's the moral? Have everything written out as fully as possible. Even if you always travel with your accompanist, a time is going to come when she's not going to be available, and you don't want to be stuck without the ability to perform your boffo arrangement.

What Not *to Sing*

A discussion of how to select audition material would be incomplete without talking about what you *shouldn't* sing. Many actors will make the mistake of choosing a song that they just adore, and that seems like an excellent audition choice in every way. Except for *them* (or at least not at this particular point in time). Your song choices should always be made with an eye toward showing off your strengths, disguising your weaknesses, and convincing the casting panel that you are right for the job.

It is extremely important that performers be able to make a valid assessment of themselves. Knowing the limits of your talents is the only way you will be able to make legitimate choices in the selection of material with which to showcase your strong points. Stretching your skills is unquestionably a commendable goal. An audition, however, is the wrong place to be experimenting.

Sarah was in the middle of her first year of her study in the Meisner Technique of acting, and taking it very seriously. She had just begun dealing with emotional preparation in her scene work. And while these studies were going on, she was continuing her vocal studies with Renèe Guerin, who also gave a weekly group audition class for her students.

For one of these classes, Sarah had readied "Where Are the Simple Joys of Maidenhood," from *Camelot.* Her emotional preparation consisted of imagining that she was pregnant and would have to give up her career. She got up in front of the group to sing and when she got to the line "Shan't I have the normal life a maiden should," she burst into hysterical tears.

Renèe (who demonstrated remarkable restraint in not rolling on the floor laughing) pointed out a valuable lesson to be learned here regarding matching an appropriate emotion to the material you are performing. In this situation Guenevere's feelings about giving up her maidenhood are more akin to the sense of loss you might feel over losing your favorite pink dress to a dry cleaning accident.

It can be interesting to turn a song on its ear by approaching it from an unusual direction, but it's a good idea to begin your work on a piece by trying to stay within the boundaries of the character and circumstance that were established in its initial theatrical setting. Or at least to be aware of those circumstances to avoid being inadvertently humorous.

Bearing this in mind, here is a list of "don'ts":

1. **Don't sing anything that is out of your range.** Material that brings you too low to be able to communicate the text is of no value to the *acting* singer. And songs that go too high, that have notes you consistently crack on, are not going to come off very well. Sometimes even when you have the notes, if they are not performed in the appropriate style, you come off badly. For example, a baritone who has a beautiful falsetto high A is going to appear foolish when he lightly sings the big final high A of a number when that note is traditionally sung full out.

2. **Don't sing material that is musically too difficult for you.** If you keep losing the beat, or you can't find your place, or you can't find your notes, *don't use the song for auditions!* (Keep working on the song until you become comfortable with it.)

3. **Don't sing material in which you are constantly aware of the technical requirements.** If you are counting the beats before your next entrance, or your mind is busy during the second verse worrying about the high note at the end of the third verse, then you will not be acting "in the moment." Any discomfort you have internally will be apparent to the casting people. Just keep working on this material away from the public eye until you feel comfortable enough to audition with it.

4. **Don't sing anything that goes on for too long.** Be aware that even in auditions where there has been no limit (like sixteen bars) imposed, the casting process is still inevitably subject to severe time constraints. Don't choose absurdly long pieces. Don't expect to sing for six straight minutes and have the panel love you for it (you'll probably be cut off anyway). Pieces like "Soliloquy" from *Carousel* and "Meadowlark" from *The Baker's Wife,* are among the finest examples of writing for the musical theatre, but they are just too long for auditions. You're better off keeping your pieces short and sweet and leaving them wanting more. If you do a good job with something brief, they'll ask for more.

   This is not to say that you can't trim down a longer song to a more reasonable length. If you do, though, try to keep your cutting artistic.

5. **Don't sing anything too boring.** This is where a good self-assessment comes in handy. Just because you personally love a piece of material doesn't mean that others won't be put to sleep by it.

Be particularly wary of
a. any song where you have thought, "I love the way the band sounds in this." (You're not going to have one.)
b. Any song that has too many identical repetitions of the same material. If a song has five melodically identical verses, you'd probably be better served doing the two or three most logical and appropriate ones and coming up with a truly sock-o ending.
c. Pop songs which, with their sometimes inscrutable lyrics, tend to have fond connotations of a purely personal nature. Be mindful of the fact that the song may not have the same connotations for the casting people as it does for you. If they can't understand the lyrics and don't know what you're talking about, you're not communicating. Be careful about being incomprehensible for too long.

6. **Don't sing anything too self-indulgent or too negative.** Material that is *too* angry, *too* bitter, *too* whiny, or *too* self-absorbed can be *too* hard to take *too* early in the morning. It should be avoided, unless, of course, the character is angry, bitter, whiny, and self-absorbed. . . . (And even then, consider carefully how *you* want to be seen.)

7. **Don't sing anything too overdone.** In the hallways outside audition rooms, one of the most commonly overheard plaints is "Oh, no! I was going to sing that."

Theoretically, if you are a stronger performer than the person who preceded you, following someone with the same material could conceivably help emphasize the difference in your talents. Unfortunately, you will automatically have to defeat the "We just heard that" feeling that the auditor may experience when they hear the introduction of your song. (Obviously, this doesn't matter if everyone is auditioning with material from the show.)

I had originally intended to include a list of overused songs, but, after looking over some of the lists that have been included in previous books on auditioning for the musical theatre, I realized that, like theirs, my list would have started down the road toward obsolescence even before this book went to press. The theatrical community is a notoriously blabby bunch. If an actor is told, "Please don't sing that. We've already heard it three times today," within days, the song has been removed from thousands of audition books. And, of course, the obverse is true (although the process is not quite so rapid): if an actor sitting outside an audition room hears an unfamiliar and interesting song being performed and thinks, "I could do that song really well," she will invariably ask the singer for the name and source of the material. The other actors in the area will hear this conversation. And they'll tell their friends, and then . . .

The best way to find out about whether a particular piece is being overutilized for auditions is to ask the people who know best. And do it early, before you've invested too much time and energy into learning it. Talk to every accompanist and person behind the table that you know. "I'm thinking of doing 'Yaditta Yaditta Yaditta.' Does that get done a lot?" But be careful who you share this information with. Don't give ideas away to the wrong people. ("Hey, my girlfriend would sound great singing 'Yaditta X 3'!")

The possibility always exists, too, that by the time you have finished preparing your newly discovered wonder and are ready to use it for auditions, it will have mysteriously passed into the area of overuse. There are no guarantees about this kind of thing. The elevator music of ten years ago could be the killer audition piece of today. And that secret discovery of today can be obsessively well-baked tomorrow.

An acquaintance of mine was friendly with someone involved with the London production of *Les Misérables* as it was just preparing to go into rehearsal. This friend had played some of the show for her during her London trip, and she asked if he could help her get a copy of one of the songs from the show. She paid for the hand preparation of the music and when she got back to the States she called me to help her get it ready for an audition for which I was already scheduled to be house accompanist.

At the audition, she came in with her music and we did a nice job with it. The director of the production asked what the song was. Generally this would be considered a coup in the selection of individualized material. Unfortunately, the next day two other women came in with the same song, from a *published* copy. This British guy had charged my friend for hand copying the music even though she could have gone to any London music store and purchased the sheet music. Somehow, overnight, this piece of specialty material had become hackneyed! Everyone was doing it.

---

8. **Don't sing anything that is too emotionally difficult for you to handle.** You don't want to lose control or go over the edge during an audition. Material that has too strong an emotional connection (at a particular point in your life) can destroy your concentration or poise.

Once upon a time, I was playing for the final exam performances of a vocal production class at the American Academy of Dramatic Arts taught by Renèe Guerin. The students were directed to behave as if attending an audition: enter the room; hand their properly prepared music to the pianist (me); convey any important information about the music to the accompanist, including tempo, repeats, etc.; introduce themselves; give a nod to the pianist; and sing their material demonstrating the techniques learned in the class.

One young woman (whom the teacher later told me had been one of her best and favorite students) came into the room and, with total poise and great concentration, demonstrated the ideal way the teacher wanted to see the audition done. Until she began to sing. Within three lines, she burst into tears and fled the room. It seems that the woman's mother had died the week before, and any lowering of her emotional barriers caused her to connect with thoughts of her mother.

Now, this is obviously an extreme example of what can happen. You should just be aware of your own public emotional limits and avoid material which will permit your feelings to interfere with your performance.[16]

9. **Don't sing anything too difficult for an average accompanist to sight-read.** It's better to uncover this in advance than to discover it during an audition. Yes, there will be times when the casting director has hired his nephew to play the auditions, and "the boy *promised* that he could play," but everything seems to be beyond him. If you are not enough of a musician to judge the difficulty of the accompaniment on your own, ask an experienced audition accompanist if the *average* accompanist could sight-read your material. At an audition, don't ever drop your music in front of the accompanist asking, "Can you play this?" This puts him on the spot and won't make him your friend. This kind of thing can come off as a dare and in an audition situation, it's better to avoid confrontation.

Once you've done the audition circuit for a while, you'll get a pretty good idea of which accompanists can play the difficult material and which ones you'd be better off giving only the "easy, big note" arrangements to. Sarah has devel-

---

16. This has no bearing on the current topic, but it's one of my favorite audition stories. This series of audition/finals seemed to be a day for bursting into tears and fleeing the room. One young lady, after doing a less than stellar job of entering the room and so on, introduced herself and her song ("Can't Help Lovin' Dat Man" from *Showboat)* and began to sing: "Birds gotta swim and fish gotta . . . gotta . . ." upon which she burst into tears and fled.

oped an inoffensive way of sounding out the abilities of accompanists who are new to her on those occasions when she is planning on doing some of her more difficult material. She'll place the music in front of the player and ask as innocently as possible, "Are you familiar with this?" If the pianist answers, "Yes," Sarah will go ahead with the song. But if the answer is anything other than a secure "Yes," she will chat about it for a moment more and then suddenly appear to change her mind: "You know, I'd really rather sing *this!*," and she'll pull out a song she feels is less challenging—without insulting the players by casting doubt about their skills. (Sorry, Sarah; now all the accompanists are on to you.)

If you feel you must bring in a song with a difficult accompaniment, it's safest to bring your own accompanist with you, someone you've rehearsed with and who you know can play it.

Be aware, also, that there is a difference between playable and sight-readable accompaniments. Some years back, it suddenly became fashionable to sing "You Must Meet My Wife" from *A Little Night Music* by Stephen Sondheim. Although it is something that I can *play,* it is very difficult to sight-read because of the enormous number of key changes and accidentals and because of the sheer quantity of rapid notes. Before I finally went out and got myself a copy of the song in order to learn it, I was—and I shudder to imply a lack of perfection in myself—caught unprepared and was forced to play several less-than-immaculate auditions. (For more on this, see Chapter 2, "Music Preparation.")

Is It Okay to Sing Original Material?

This question always makes me laugh. Does this mean that "I Feel Pretty" from *West Side Story*, and "My Heart Is So Full of You" from *The Most Happy Fella*, and "Where is Love?" from *Oliver* are not original?

The term "original" music usually refers to unpublished songs composed by unknown writers. The fact that they are unknown is not, of course, automatically a reflection on their abilities as writers. Every successful writer was unknown at some time and thus was guilty of writing "original" music. But some unknown writers are deservedly so and will perhaps always remain writers of "original" music.

The question boils down to this: "Is this piece of 'original' music good enough and appropriate enough, and will it allow me to give a successful audition?" As we've seen throughout this chapter, the selection of your audition material is a serious, reflective, and careful process. You must scrutinize the "original" material as thoroughly as you would regular published material. Does it fulfill the requirements demanded of audition material? You will have to remove your blinders very carefully when you try to answer this question. Don't let your affection for the writer or the material interfere with your objectivity. Scrutinize yourself: if you can't be objective, don't do the material. An audition is not the best place to showcase someone's song anyway (even if it's your own). You're there to showcase yourself!

I Was in the Right Place, but It Must've Been . . .

In our slightly less than best of all possible worlds, an actor will occasionally be called in to audition for a role for which she is completely wrong. A woman friend of mine became infuriated with her agent. She had been signed with this man for several years and had booked many shows through him, which would seem to indicate that he should have had a pretty good idea of who she was and what kind of roles she should be sent up for. Her anger on this occasion was the result of her agent having gotten her an audition for the tough, tomboyish gamin role of "Anybodys" in a production of *West Side Story*. My friend, however, is especially well endowed and is notorious for her sex appeal. What could this agent have been thinking?

When this happens, before you cancel the appointment out of hand, carefully examine the possible benefits of attending the audition. Even though there is no way you can see yourself playing this role:

1. Is it possible that the production team has a different take on the role than the traditional one or the published breakdown?
2. Is there another role that the casting panel, after having seen you, might conceivably consider you for?
3. Is it important enough that these people see you for future consideration?

If the answer to any of these questions is yes, then the standards for the selection of material which we have established in this chapter need to be adjusted to take into account a slightly different set of goals. The bottom line of showing yourself to your best advantage remains paramount, but the appropriateness of the material is no longer as important. By all means, *try* to be appropriate to the character, the show, and the music—but not at the expense of your personal image. Do not demean yourself by trying to pull off a characterization, a style, or even a vocal range that you know is beyond you. Go in there, be a wonderful performer, sing your most brilliant audition material and get out! Leave it to them to sort out the details. If you do well, they'll discern your aptness for another role in the show or another show, or they'll file your picture and resume for future consideration. You don't need to help them—your sole job is to come off brilliantly.

If, on the other hand, there seems to be no reason at all to attend the audition, by all means cancel the appointment. Make sure that the reason for the cancellation is explained (and do it gracefully). Never just fail to appear at an audition for any reason.

Sarah had gone through a series of auditions for a European tour of *My Fair Lady.* She was up for the part of Eliza, a role she has long wanted to play. One morning, about a week after her final callback, she received a phone call from her manager's office: "You're going to have trouble believing this, but the *My Fair Lady* people called with an offer. They want you to understudy Eliza and play the role of Freddy." "What!!?!" (There is no form of punctuation which can adequately describe her actual response.) John Woodward, one of the people at the management agency Sarah is signed with, had assiduously questioned the casting people who insisted that this *was* the offer. Sarah asked that he please just check with them again. (Freddy, by the way, is the young man in the play who is courting Eliza. He sings "On The Street Where You Live.")

About an hour later, the phone rang and I answered it. It was John again. He said that the casting people were starting to sound a little angry and had demanded, "Does she want the role or not?" They confirmed that this was indeed the offer, but they had attempted to clarify the offer by explaining that she would be playing "Freddy in a gray wig." This was even more confusing—what kind of production was this going to be anyway? Were they expecting Sarah to dress as a man or were they planning on Eliza's suitor being played as an elderly woman? Sarah and I decided that if the casting people were going to be this stupid, we would play along—after all, a contract is a contract. If they signed it as drawn up to read that Sarah would play Freddy, it would cost them big when they figured out their error.

I told John to tell the casting people that Sarah would be delighted to accept under the following conditions: (1) that she be the one to select the key for her song; (2) that since she would be playing one principal role and understudying another, she would be paid an amount no less than one-and-a-half times the salary of the highest paid principal; and (3) that her chest would not be "bound."

Several hours went by and John called to say that the casting people had called. They sheepishly admitted that there had been an error and that the offer was for the Eliza understudy and "Mrs. Eynsford-Hill in a gray wig" (Freddy's mother).

(Sarah chose to pass, telling them that it was Freddy or nothing. She was a little disappointed, though; she would have sounded great singing "On The Street Where You Live.")

The Sixteen-Bar (or Less) Limit

Be forewarned: This section involves math (I'll be doing it all, so don't panic) and, no, the title does not refer to rules of organized barhopping. This is a restriction that you will usually come up against in open calls (also referred to as *cattle calls*) and Eligible Performer Principal Auditions. Because of time limitations, coupled with an often overwhelmingly large turnout, the casting people will often find it necessary to ask that the auditionees limit themselves to singing only sixteen measures of a song. With the application of a little math, the reasons become obvious.

The sixth-grade word problem would look something like this

> If a casting call is scheduled for eight hours in one day, say 10:00 A.M. to 6:00 P.M., and if by 10:00 A.M. the sign-up sheet contains 200 names, how much time is available for each person's audition?

THE ANSWER

Assuming that all external factors have miraculously been controlled (*e.g.*, all necessary members of the casting team have arrived at the audition at the appropriate time, the vagaries of the public transportation system have been surmounted, all necessary paperwork has been remembered, the check to pay for the audition room was brought, the accompanist has arrived, all of the breakfast orders have been taken in a timely fashion, and all of the appropriate planets are in the correct alignment) and things start on time, and the casting team has decided on taking a single hour for lunch, that leaves seven hours, or 420 minutes for the audition.

Now, if the monitor is absolutely together and ushers people in and out of the room at a constant and steady rate, and if all of the actors are completely prepared and they don't spend too much time chatting with the casting team, and if they bring everything they need into the room (picture and resume, songs, and appropriate footwear), and barring any other natural and unnatural obstruction to this perfectly functioning audition machine we are imagining, we'd have to allow at least a minute-and-a-half per person to get into the room, talk to the accompanist, introduce themselves, and get out. So, 1.5 minutes times 200 people equals 300 minutes—that's five hours! Which leaves only two hours for singing! But, okay, let's really shoot for perfection: Let's knock the time for the extras down to a single minute (we'll pretend that the room is small, the walk to the piano is a short one, and that communication with the pianist is always without problem). That's only three hours and twenty minutes for entrances and exits, leaving us with 220 minutes, or 3 hours and 40 minutes for the actual audition part. So, if there are not going to be any monologues heard, and the casting people are able to tell all they need to from a single song, in order to hear all 200 people, each song will have to be no more than one minute and six seconds long (220 minutes divided by 200 people).

But, you know what? As any garden-variety scientist would tell you, this kind of perfection is only achievable in mathematical models. And, let's face it, would you want to be Number 200 walking into the room at 5:58 P.M. (and 14 seconds) to face a group that has given itself this kind of restrictive schedule to maintain? How much of an impression can you make on a panel whose bladders are bursting and whose brains have turned to cottage cheese?

Let's move the model into the real world (and be aware that even some of these deductions are unreasonably modest)

The Deductions	Running Tally
▪ The full audition day (8 hours)	480 min.
▪ One hour lunch	420 min.
▪ The accompanist shows up seven minutes late and takes three minutes to get settled.	410 min.

- The casting director panicked when the accompanist was not there and has run out of the room to find a phone to call her. Once the accompanist arrives, the casting director cannot be found, and the panel waits for her return. After a few minutes they decide to go ahead without her. But we've still lost another 5 minutes. — 405 min.

- The casting director returns and apologizes. The accompanist apologizes to the casting director. (2 minutes) — 403 min.

- The artistic director makes a speech about how much time has been lost and how they have to work more quickly now. (3 minutes) — 400 min.

- Let's give them an average of 5 minutes every hour to stretch and use the bathroom. (5 minutes x 8 hours = 40 minutes) — 360 min.

- Out of the 200 people, only 12 forget to bring in their picture and resume. Thirty seconds each to run out of the room, dig through their bags, find the picture and resume, and run back in. (30 seconds x 12 people = 6 minutes) — 354 min.

- Of those 12, four realize that they didn't bring a picture and resume. An additional 30 seconds each for making excuses. (30 seconds x 4 people = 2 minutes) — 352 min.

- Only twice during the day are the auditions interrupted by phone calls to the choreographer. (5 minutes x 2 = 10 minutes) — 342 min.

- The casting panel has decided to have lunch from 1:00 to 2:00 P.M. In order to save time, rather than go out, they are going to have lunch brought in. They manage to take the orders without interrupting the schedule and the monitor calls it in for them. The lunch arrives at 12:40. (10 minutes to accept the order and figure out payment) — 332 min.

- One out of 20 actors excites debate about her relative value and merit. (1 minute each x 10 people = 10 minutes) — 322 min.
- Fifteen people have not read this book and have come in with their music improperly prepared. Add one additional minute per person. (15 minutes) — 307 min.
- Twenty actors are asked to sing an additional 30 seconds of ballad each (30 seconds, plus 15 seconds to find the song and communicate with the pianist x 20 people = 15 minutes) — 292 min.
- Ten of these people aren't fully prepared to sing a second song and take an average additional 30 seconds to find it. (5 minutes) — 287 min.
- Four of these people didn't bring any other music into the room and have to leave to get it. (An average additional 45 seconds each = 3 minutes) — 284 min.
- Our standard one-minute deduction per person for entrance and exit. (200 minutes) — 84 min.

Eighty-four minutes for 200 people to sing in! Too bad the auditions aren't for a choir—everyone could sing for more than an hour. But since we're looking at individuals here, let's see, um . . ., 84 minutes divided by 200 people equals .42 minutes or 25.2 seconds. Less than a half-minute per person of singing. And 25, okay (we'll give them less time in the bathroom) 26 seconds at 120 beats per minute equals 52 beats or, in 4/4 time, 13 measures of music.

(After all this math, I have to go lie down. Talk quietly among yourselves. I'll be back.)

Okay, so with our careful mathematical study, we can see that a sixteen-bar limit is almost frivolously generous. And, by the way, I've been involved with By Appointment Auditions where only six to eight people are scheduled per hour (7.5 to 10 minutes each) that have fallen an hour behind by lunch time!

So, now that we see that there are sound (and mathematically based) reasons for a sixteen-bar limit (and that it is not merely the evil creation of a diabolically insensitive casting director embittered by her lack of success as an actor), what on earth can be done in sixteen measures, or about thirty-two seconds?

The Well-Prepared Sixteen

You should always bear in mind that if the request is made to limit your song to sixteen bars, then time is considered at a premium. Having everything completely prepared in advance and giving every consideration to trimming the fat from every aspect of your audition—in short, behaving in a fully professional manner—will gain you bonus points in the eyes of the people holding the casting session. You will be judged from the minute you enter the room and you don't want the panel to think you are wasting their time.

- **Have your sixteen-bar pieces prepared in advance.** Do not go into the room expecting to make the decision on the spot with the accompanist. Choices made at the last minute will rarely be as effective as preparations made in advance. When I've been asked during an audition to help make cuts to fit the sixteen-bar limit, I've *tried* to be helpful and look for the meat of the song, but because of the time pressures it was not possible to devote more than a few seconds to these choices. Often I've felt compelled to simply count backward from the final double bar. And I guarantee that that's not the best way to make this kind of decision.

  Your sixteen-bar song should be as carefully planned as your regular full-length pieces. You have the same goals to achieve in perhaps a quarter of the time. But, also be aware that a good sixteen-bar selection is more like a movie preview: you want to whet the interest of the casting panel and excite them to want to hear more.

  I have a friend who always uses the same piece of material when confronted with a sixteen-bar limit. It's so effective that sometimes he uses it even when there isn't this kind of restriction. And it's only eleven measures long! This impressively edited little masterpiece allows him to show off—there's some quick patter-y stuff, some sustained *melodic* singing, and some bluesy wailing.

  While no one expects this kind of arranging to occur for a sixteen-bar piece of music, prepreparation is essential.

Choose your sixteen bars as carefully as you choose your full-length pieces. Try to achieve at least a small amount of shape, with highs and lows of musical and emotional lines. And don't always assume that the final section of a song will be the best portion—sometimes the middle part will be more effective than the end.

- **Make sure the selection has some sense of completion.** Don't be singing along nicely, tra-la-la-la-la, hold for a be-yoot-i-ful fat note, and then in the middle of the phrase, stop and say, "That's sixteen measures!" That can be good for a laugh once in a while, but it's less effective than a well-thought-out piece of material that at least *tries* to cadence satisfactorily.
- **No, the introduction doesn't count as part of the sixteen bars.** Usually. Oh, you may get some jerk one day who wants to argue the point, but that will be extremely rare. In such an instance, say "Fine!" and just ask for your starting note. Jerks are no rarity in this business. You can gloat on your superiority after you leave the room. You should know your material well enough to begin from just the starting note.

Non-Equity actors are subjected to all kinds of absurd indignities that make the sixteen-bar limitation seem like generosity. During Sarah's early non-Equity days, at an audition for a "new" Gershwin revue, the monitor announced to the waiting actors that they would be seen in groups of five. Five actors would enter the room and perform their audition pieces, one after another. When the final actor had sung, they would all leave. This meant that each would have to listen to the others' auditions. (This type of insensitivity is not all that uncommon in the non-Equity world.)

When they entered the room, they were introduced to the rather elderly man behind the piano, who, it was explained, was acting as accompanist for the auditions, although he was also the director, musical director, and arranger. The first of the group, a young Black woman, had prepared a type of ethnic movement to go along with her song. After a few bars, the man stopped playing and yelled, "Could you just do it without all that crap!" He began playing again, and, although she tried, it seems that the movement was just too integrated into her performance for her to abandon it entirely. "Listen, honey. Why don't you just stop? Go out in the hall and think about it. If you can't do it without all that garbage going on, then just leave!"

The next woman came up and a few bars into the song, he laid into her about something involving her vocal production. After a few attempts and a lot more abuse, she left the room in tears.

The next two did not fare much better. Sarah was last, and by the time she got up to sing, she had reached the limits of her patience. Sure enough, a few bars into the song he stopped. "Can't you do it without that obnoxious vibrato?"

Sarah grabbed her music and spit out, "No, I can't" and tore out of the room.

The woman who had been sent out of the room to think about her extraneous movements asked Sarah's advice. "Should I go back in there?" Sarah said, "No. He's an imbecile. If the best you can expect from this audition is the opportunity to work with a geriatric idiot like him, why bother?" A group of women who had been sent out of the room for one reason or another heard this and burst into spontaneous applause.

The monitor grabbed Sarah's arm. "Don't you know who he is? You better go back and apologize. He's a very successful and highly regarded man!" Sarah yanked her arm away and shouted, "Yeah? Well, when I reach my peak, he'll be dead!"

If you remember that you are being limited to sixteen bars primarily because of time constraints, deciding you need an eight-bar piano solo introduction to your sixteen bars in order to "set the mood" is sheer insanity. Reducing a four- or eight-bar intro to one or two bars is a good idea. Often a simple bell-tone *("puh-link")* or an arpeggio *("baah-labalabalabalaba-laba-link")* is enough to get you started. If you can't determine these things on your own, make sure you work them out with an accompanist.

▪ **Bonus Bars!!!** Here is a tiny secret: Only once in my entire career have I heard of a monomaniacal lunatic who insists on counting the prepared number of bars of the auditionees before letting them sing. So it is entirely probable that you will be permitted a little bit of flexibility in your actual total bar count. But I don't guarantee anything, and for heaven's sake, don't go telling anyone I said it was okay!

I came about this determination through a simple premise: we know that the sixteen-bar limit is imposed because of time constraints. When a casting agent imposes this requirement, it means that she is willing to hear singing for a finite amount of time.

16 measures x 4 beats per measure = 64 beats
120 beats per minute = 2 beats per second
64 divided by 2 = 32 seconds

Therefore, we can deduce that a casting director is essentially stating that she is willing to hear a selection lasting approximately thirty seconds.

So, if your song is in an average tempo $\frac{2}{4}$ meter (120 beats

"I know they said 'your best 16 bars,' but they're really pressed for time, so now they only want to hear your best one note."

per minute, or bpm), you can more than likely get away with thirty-two bars since you will encounter twice the number of bars in the same amount of time as a $\frac{4}{4}$ song in the same tempo. Or the same number of bars in a quick cut-time ($\mathbb{C}$ $\bigm|$ = **120** or faster). Or, for something in a moderately paced $\frac{3}{4}$ time, you could conceivably go as long as twenty-one measures. And if the request is for sixteen bars of a ballad, we're looking at something more like 45 seconds.

But, hey, you don't need to take out your slide rule or calculator to figure out the actual appropriate length of your sixteen-bar song. It's better to take a more artistic approach: find a song you think will work for you and pare it down to its most essential elements. Start with, perhaps, a single phrase. Time that phrase. Let's say you got twenty seconds—not bad, and if that phrase by itself works artistically, leave it alone. Always err on the shorter side. But if there is another half-phrase that will increase the quality of the presentation, then find a way to connect it—artistically.

Let's look at an easy example. The song "I Met A Girl" by Betty Comden, Adolph Green, and Jule Styne, from the musical, *Bells Are Ringing*, is in ¢ time and is generally performed at somewhere between $\quarternote = 140$ and $\quarternote = 164$. If we look at a single verse, from "I met a girl . . ." through "Hey, what am I getting so excited about," we see that the phrase length is exactly 16 measures long. 16 measures of 2 beats per measure at 140 bpm will run about 13.7 seconds. This leaves plenty of time. So let's look at the final appearance of the verse. This adds a coda (from "I met a girl . . ." through ". . . and I fell in love today.") which comes to a total of twenty-four bars, with a good shape and a nice, big, fat, final note. And all in about 20.6 seconds. Which means that adding two or even four measures of the introduction is no problem (.9 seconds for two bars or 1.8 seconds for four).

Be careful if the breakdown calls for sixteen bars of only an up-tempo exclusively; this generally will mean that they'll be expecting songs upward of our 120 bpm estimation tempo. Which means they'll be expecting you to be singing for less than the 30 seconds we've been discussing. If the request is for sixteen bars each of an up-tempo and a ballad, you have even more leeway. But don't feel like you can whip open a twenty-page accordion-folded arrangement across the piano and get away with it.

- **Never, ever, ever, ever just start a song at the beginning and plan on going as far as you can.** This lack of preparation looks extremely unprofessional and, in fact, does an enormous disservice to you. You inevitably will be cut off, and usually not very politely. You won't like it, and I can guarantee you that the casting panel won't like it. In fact, there have been occasions when I was playing for auditions and was told by the people running the audition to warn actors that I had been instructed to simply stop playing after sixteen measures if they were planning to go beyond that limit (I would allow for fast tempos and for $\frac{2}{4}$ or $\frac{3}{4}$ time). (Standing outside of an audition room, I once overheard the introduction to "Tonight" frm *West Side Story* being played. Then "Tonight. . . ." "Thank you! Next!")

- **An eight-bar limit is rare**, but not unheard of in non-Equity calls. Deal with this in the most artistic way you can. I'm really sorry; it's an awful thing. (I once played a day of auditions for a notoriously cranky artistic director who, when he felt we had not seen enough people yet that day, imposed a four-bar limit!)

More Sixteen-Bar Rambling

Your 16-bar material does not necessarily have to be chosen from your full-length pieces. It is possible that you may discover that sixteen measures of a particular song will work for you even though you would never think of singing the entire song.

Oh, and by the way, if you are ever asked, "Can you sing a little bit of something else?", consider *a little bit* to be a euphemism meaning "sixteen bars."

Try to think of the sixteen-bar limit not as an unfair restriction, but more as an artistic challenge. Remember what my friend was able to get out of his mere eleven measures. And also think about the fact that if not for the imposed sixteen-bar limit, there might not be enough time one day to squeeze your audition in.

And, finally, Sarah insists that I promise those of you who are forced to submit to the indignity of cattle-call sixteen-bar limits that some day in your future, things will get better. By Appointment Auditions can be downright pleasant!

A Note About Finding Songs

Actually finding material to sing for auditions is one of the most challenging parts of an actor's life. There are coaches who specialize in matching obscure material to an actor's talents, but finding such a coach is not a necessity.

Most actors find their songs by always keeping their ears open. When you go to see a show, keep your search for new material in the back of your mind. Is that big ballad in the second act right for you? All over the country, there are radio stations with shows that specialize in musical theatre programming. Listen to them! Even elevators and supermarkets with piped-in music can spark an idea.

Hit your local library, or find one with a good selection of recordings and music. Check out all the material you can, survey it, digest it, analyze it, and then figure out how it can be plundered for your needs.

Rent every musical you can find on video.

The best place of all to both find and develop new material is in a repertoire class. These are often given by voice teachers, coaches, or directors. Students get up in front of the group and perform whatever piece(s) they are currently working on. The performers then receive impressions and direction from the teacher, and sometimes from the class as well. But of most value is the fact that the instructor recommends new material and the student will be exposed to songs recommended to the others.

To help you develop a well-rounded repertory, I've included a guide to creating a complete audition book (see Appendix A).

The Bottom Line

Whatever you end up singing, know your material. And know it well, backward and forward. You should be able to sing it *a cappella* and still stay in tune and rhythm. You should be able to sing it despite an "accompanist's" best efforts to stop you. Know it so well that even, for example, the sudden explosion of the casting director's head wouldn't make you lose your place.

Paul Ford, who has played for many Stephen Sondheim shows from preproduction through production, was playing a day of auditions when a very young Japanese woman brought him a brand-spanking-new copy of the sheet music for "I Cain't Say No," obviously just purchased from a music shop around the corner from the auditions. Paul tried to coax some information from her about the tempo and repeats and such, but she was rather timid and her English limited. He told her to nod when she was ready and helped her find a place to stand.

She nodded to him and he began the introduction. When it came time for her to sing she ran over to him and stopped him. She asked him to play the intro again so she could hear it, which he did. She then returned to her place, nodded, and after the intro began: "When I have a brand-new hairdo . . .," the lyrics to "I Enjoy Being A Girl," from *Flower Drum Song*. Right writers, wrong song. Paul didn't know how to react, so he kept playing. And she kept singing the wrong lyrics. Despite the error, believe it or not, things kept working out until the middle section when it all finally fell apart. Paul stopped playing and the woman looked around, perplexed. Since no one quite knew what to do, they thanked her for her time and she left.

The only way you can feel comfortable is if you know your material well enough not to be distracted by it. And you can't act unless you feel comfortable. And if you don't care about the acting, then maybe the musical theatre is not the best place for your talents (although I could tell you some stories . . .).

The Audition— 5
The Who
and the How

S hortly after our wedding, Sarah and I were subjected to a particularly hellish I.R.S. audit. It was
(obviously) our first joint return and we were up
against a junior auditor who had no experience
with an arts related return:

Auditor: What are all these transportation expenses for?
Sarah: That's for going to auditions.
Auditor: An audition? An audition? What's that? Like an
audit?
Steve: No. It's like a job interview to be in a play.
Auditor: So, wait. Let me get this straight. According to
your datebook, how many audits do you go to?
Sarah: *Auditions!* And, I don't know, between three and
five a week, maybe.
Steve: Maybe one hundred and fifty a year.
Auditor: So, you're telling me that you go on one hundred and
fifty job interviews a year and you don't have a job yet?

Just the kind of thing a painfully struggling actress
needs to hear. (Don't worry, though—it ended up costing
the I.R.S. a lot more to do the audit than they got from us.)
The general, nontheatre population has little, if any,
understanding of what occurs at an audition, and even the

people involved have some serious misconceptions. There are two tiny but enormously important points that many auditioning actors continually forget and in forgetting them, cause themselves unnecessary stress. The knowledge of these secrets will greatly enhance your understanding of the audition process. Are you prepared?

They concern

The People Behind the Table

Okay, this is it. The first secret is that the people behind the casting table *are just people!* Yup. That's it. (Shhhh! We don't want everyone to know.) Sitting there may be the Queen of the Play and the King of Casting, but these are not positions that have been bestowed by divine right. They are just people, with the same foibles and emotions that everyone else is subject to. They have usually achieved their station through hard work and effort (just like you're trying to do), which is, presumably, the same way the president of a corporation, a traffic cop, and the manager of the local Wendy's achieved their positions of authority.

You may come up against a very snooty, conceited director who seems to look upon you with disdain. But that kind of behavior shouldn't be totally unfamiliar to you. We've all come up against a mere mortal somewhere in our pasts who has exhibited the same sort of behavior. (I remember having some trouble with my junior high school football coach—"You may be fast, but I don't know if there's room on this here team for a music sissy!")

Deal with the people behind the table in the same way you would deal with any person in authority (when in doubt, think bellicose traffic cop). If you audition for someone who exhibits signs of antisocial behavior, someone who instantly seems to hate you, be gracious, be charming, be a better person than he is. Don't fight him because you can't win. (Remember what I said about traffic cops?) And if it seems to be a no-win situation, be aware that there is no longer anyone in the industry who has the power to follow through on the old threat, "You'll never work in this town again!"

Okay, here comes the other secret that will really help you through the trauma of auditions. (Lean closer; I don't want *everyone* to hear.) Are you ready? They *want* you to be good; they're hoping you're good; their greatest desire is for you to be exactly

The People Behind the Casting Table:
Sleeping Man and Eating Man

what their show needs. That's the reason for the audition in the first place: to find a bunch of actors to fill a bunch of roles. And if you have prepared properly and seem to meet their needs, then they are going to want to give you the job, or at least call you back in for another look.

So, those are them: the two most important ideas in this book. Everything you do for your auditions should be with these two thoughts in mind: no matter what they seem, the casting people are just people and they want you to be the answer to their casting needs.

Your Assignment

Your main job, above any other consideration, is to make a good impression. The people behind the table will be making value judgments about you—as an actor *and* as a person. They will be judging you constantly, from the moment you walk in the door. Whatever happens in the room, when it's all over you want them to remember you as a potential asset. So you want to present the best possible image the entire time you're under their examination. Here are some tips.

- **Dress neatly, or appropriately.** Just as the selection of an appropriate song is important in cluing the casting people in to your suitability for a role, your choice of outfit can also be an invaluable asset. Unless you want to be remembered as a slob or a perpetual adolescent, avoid ripped jeans and t-shirts when auditioning for more mainstream roles. By the same token, though, a suit and tie are probably the wrong things to wear for an audition for a Jet in *West Side Story*.

New York City is not a great place to walk around in beautiful shoes, so many actresses travel to their auditions wearing sneakers and carrying their pumps in their audition bags.

Sarah arrived at her audition for the New York company of *Nunsense* and discovered that she had forgotten to put her shoes in her bag. So she had to walk out onto the stage of the Douglas Fairbanks Theater wearing a beautiful dress and a beat-up pair of Reeboks. She handed her music to the accompanist and walked out to center stage.

"I'm sooo embarrassed. I have to tell you how really sorry I am about the sneakers. I forgot to bring my shoes."

Joe Abaldo, the casting director, and Dan Goggin, the creator/director, burst out laughing, and after a second Sarah realized why.

She was auditioning for the role of Sister Amnesia.

(She got the job and played the role off-Broadway over a period of two years.)

There are some people who, when they go to extremes of dressiness, look uncomfortable (you know who you are). Men don't have to wear suits or sports coats and ties, and women don't have to wear ball gowns or cocktail dresses (unless the role calls for it, of course). Dress neatly, nicely, comfortably, and flatteringly. Think "casual dressy."

Remember, too, that you are there to sell yourself. Don't be afraid to show off. This is the theatre we're talking about, not a corporate board meeting. Your physical assets are part of the total package, so flaunting them is not something you should avoid.

- **Behave well.** Be adult and professional. Unless you have friends in the room—say, you've had a good rehearsal experience with the choreographer—don't try to be too friendly. You don't need to shake everyone's hand. Treat it like business.
- **Prepare an "audition briefcase."** This can be any handy totable bag—a shopping bag, a knapsack, a shoulder bag, an oversized purse, a gym bag, etc. Into this bag place everything you could possibly need for an audition: pictures and resumes, your music, monologues, your tap shoes, and anything else that could conceivably be needed at an audition. This bag will go with you to every audition, thus assuring that, like the best boy scout, you will always be prepared.

- And, **take charge.** Help keep the audition moving. Make sure your songs are easily accessible. If they are in a book, enter the room with the book opened to the appropriate page or marked with a taped-on paper flag. If you help keep things on track, the casting people will be thankful. Always try to anticipate what they will want next. A ballad? You've got it ready to go. And speaking of which . . .

More *About the Song*

Do you remember what we said your song needs to do? I'll remind you. First, it has to show you off to your best advantage; and, second, it should be appropriate. Try to find out in advance— from the breakdown in the trade papers, your manager, or your agent—what they are asking for. At the very least, check with the monitor *before* you go into the room. As a matter of fact, it's a good idea to double check with the monitor even if you did get your information in advance. There's nothing quite like preparing a massive, full-length selection and being told, once you've given your music to the piano player, that they'd only like to hear sixteen bars, please.

Find out if they are

- Listening to up-tempos and/or ballads;
- Hearing full-length songs or just (sixteen-bar) selections.

If you haven't been able to find out which specifically they'd like to hear—or if they haven't expressed a preference—then once you've gone in there it's okay to ask, "Would you prefer an up-tempo or a ballad?" *But*, if they have not made any preference known, then you don't *have* to ask. If *your* preference is for one or the other, then definitely sing your stronger material first. (Yes, your up-tempo and your ballad should be equally strong, but you may be more comfortable with one than the other.) And don't ask, "Are you going to hear more than one song?" Assume that you need to sell them with the first one. If they want to hear more, there's nothing to stop them from asking for it.

Sometimes the panel will want to hear something other than what you have initially prepared. Perhaps the song has been heard once too often, or they don't feel that it's appropriate, or someone there just hates it. It's a good idea to have some back-ups in mind. This is a time when a nice thick book of audition repertoire can come in handy. But . . .

WARNING! Occasionally, when a situation like this arises, the accompanist, the musical director, or someone will want to leaf through your material to "help" come up with a song choice. For this reason, you don't *ever* want to go into an audition room with material you're not prepared to sing.

A very dear friend of mine, whom we'll call "Louise Cassou," is well known for her work on the "legitimate" stage. She is in constant demand for productions around the country. Like many classically trained actors, she has a remarkable singing voice with a very wide range and she has done quite a few musicals. But because she auditions for musicals so rarely, she's not as confident in her abilities as she should be and is scrupulous about preparing her material, spending extensive amounts of time being coached on the songs, and practicing conscientiously.

She was up for a role in a production of *Anything Goes,* and she had been told that she would not need to sing at her first appointment.

Things were going fine at the audition: the reading had gone well and a friendly discussion followed about her previous performances. Then, horror of horrors, the casting director said, "Well, I know we didn't ask for it, but could you just sing us a little something?"

Lou had just begun preparing for the singing audition. She had picked up a copy of "Baby Face" and had spent some time coaching with her husband, who had warned her to be especially careful of the rhythm at the end of the first phrase, ". . . you sure have started something." Nonetheless, she did not yet feel adequately prepared to sing. And she told them so.

By unfortunate coincidence, her bag was open on the floor near her, and visible to the casting director was her copy of "Baby Face." "Why don't you just sing a little of that?"

"No . . . I couldn't! I don't know it . . . I'm not comfortable singing it yet. I'm really not ready to. . ."

"Oh, come on. Don't worry about it! We just want to hear a little. And you can hold the music!"

She got talked into it. So there she stood, music rattling in her shaking hands, trying to get through her song. Since she was holding the music and the accompanist couldn't fake it, she had to sing it *a cappella.*

She was doing fine until she got to the end of the first phrase, when suddenly her husband's warning popped into her head. Now there was no chance that she'd sing it correctly.

So the audition that had begun so positively ended badly. All because a little bit of music was peeking out of her bag.

Don't carry material that you're just learning, or that you've just picked up to learn, or that your girlfriend asked you to buy for her, with your regular audition material. If it ends up in the audition room it can end up being used against you. I've seen some very persuasive force used to get actors to do material they're not prepared to do, and usually with unpleasant results. You don't need to end up in a discussion about why you can't perform a particular piece of material, either.

Doctor, My Eye . . .

A big question I get is "Where should I look during my song?" or "What should I do with my eyes?"

This is another one of those questions for which there is no clear-cut answer. You should think of your audition as a variation of a stage performance. All of the rules, methods, and concepts that come into play when planning a stage performance must be brought to bear when working out your audition performance. Unlike any other form of stage performance, however, you are trapped in a tiny room and are standing only feet away from your audience.

In a musical you would rarely assume direct eye contact with a member of the audience. You'd be more likely to make contact with another character, or, in the case of an interior-monologue type of song, you might have more of a generalized audience focus.

You will have to use your judgment and acting skills to figure out how to use your eyes. Instinct will also come into play. Try to feel out your audience (the auditors). If you have planned to have all kinds of fun and contact with the people behind the table, but you walk into the room and immediately sense that you've walked into a meeting of the "Surly Society," change your plans. I have been on casting panels where certain members prefer to have direct contact made and others were made uncomfortable by it. Some find it an opportunity to do battle, like the kid's challenge of who-will-turn-away-first. This is another situation where you really don't need to end up in a contest of egos. (Save that for the rehearsals!)

The ultimate decision regarding what to do with your eyes should be motivated by the song. What do the situation, character, and emotion suggest? Is this an intimate scene between lovers? Then there should be the appearance of intimate contact with another character. Is it a rabble-rousing diatribe? Then, of course, the focus should be more generalized, more presentational. Let the actor in you make the ultimate decision.

A good general rule is to pick points a few inches above each of the auditors' heads. If you are dealing with other characters in your scene, imagine them to be sitting or moving on a raised platform behind the casting people.

And make sure that you shift focus occasionally. Don't become locked and develop dead eyes—the deer-in-the-head-lights syndrome which many young actors fall prone to. Getting hung up staring at a single point makes you look panic stricken or zombie-like. (Of course, if you're auditioning for the musical version of *Night of the Living Dead,* you'll be all set.) Besides, shifting focus has the effect of sharing your face with different members of the panel.

I suggest that you avoid making direct eye contact, except very occasionally. Direct contact in songs that contain the equivalent of asides can be particularly effective, but avoid using eye contact as an assault or a challenge.

Uh-Oh, or, the Boo-Boo

Hey, it happens: you forget the words, the accompanist misunderstands the music, a fire alarm goes off in the studio. Something occurs to destroy the smooth flow of your audition. And you want to die.

Whatever happens, don't panic. Remember—you are under constant scrutiny the entire time you're in the room. Everyone makes mistakes and a graceful recovery from a train wreck can actually make you look good!

Since Sarah had recently done some work for one of the producers of *Jerry's Girls,* we were invited to a preview performance.

In one of the numbers, Dorothy Louden appeared from stage left, dressed in a Shirley Temple outfit, with a little tiny dress, many petticoats, a bow in her hair, and a giant lollipop. She skipped merrily across the stage, opened her mouth to sing, and showed some obvious consternation when all that emerged were several nonsense syllables. She stopped and turned to the conductor: "I messed up. Can we do it again?" She turned to the audience and said: "Well, it *is* a preview!"

The audience howled. And everyone adored her for it—not just for her absolute cuteness, but for letting us in on the process of creating a show, and for her candor in revealing her fallibility.

"Do you mind if I stop until the UFOs have landed and Elvis has left the building?"

Always try to recover without stopping, if it's at all possible. If, for example, you inadvertently shift to the second-verse lyrics halfway through the first verse of your song, could you conceivably switch to the first-verse lyrics halfway through the second? I've seen quite a few fairly well-known performers lose track of their lyrics in the middle of an audition and recover with some versatile ad-libbing.

If you miss an entrance, try to get back in gracefully, if possible. Some accompanists are attentive enough to recognize that this has occurred and will create a kind of on-the-spot vamp for you (which hopefully you'll recognize as such). But, unfortunately, you can't count on that.

You should only stop if

1. the pianist has gone completely astray;
2. you are irreparably lost; or
3. something so dreadful occurs that you cannot possible recover from it.

Sometimes, for no apparent reason, the accompanist will misunderstand your instructions or something about the music itself. He may start out at double time or have forgotten to look at the key signature and be playing your minor key song in a very odd-sounding major key. By all means, stop before the introduction is over and go over and explain the error of his ways.

If you have completely lost your way, or something unrecoverable has happened, resume professionally. You don't really have to ask if it's all right to fix the problem—the need will more than likely be obvious (and if it isn't, you shouldn't have stopped in the first place!). You need to remember about the time crunch and try to keep things moving, even while you're trying to take care of the quality of your audition.

Unless you are very near the beginning, don't start the song over. Turn to the pianist and say: "Can we take it from the second 'Can't we stop for a moment' [or wherever] and could you just give me the two bars before it to get me in?" Then, if it seems like the right thing to do, you can apologize after the number is over. Often you'll find that this is not even necessary.

If for any reason you find that you will have to be late for, or will have to miss a scheduled appointment entirely, do your best to get in touch with the casting people (or have your agent or manager do it for you). Call the casting agent's office or the rehearsal studio itself. Keep it professional—if you do, there is the possibility of rescheduling your appointment. If you stand them up without explanation, they are bound to be insulted and you may have trouble getting future auditions through them. (Casting directors, like elephants, are known for their remarkable memories.)

You'll discover that audition days rarely keep to their planned schedule (as explained in the previous chapter). The morning is usually more on track than the afternoon, of course. And then there are the bizarre days when casting people, for reasons known only to them, call in eight or ten people at the same time. That means somebody is going to be kept waiting.

But even though you will rarely be seen at the actual time of your appointment, don't count on any sort of time cushion. The one time you say, "I'm not worried, they're always late," will be the time that the three appointments before yours are cancelled and now the auditions are *ahead* of schedule. And *you'll* be the one who's remembered as being late. Most casting directors will build some kind of latitude into the schedule in order to try to keep things on track. It's better for you to sit waiting in the lounge than for them to have to wait for your arrival.

A Short Guide to Hallway Etiquette

You've schlepped your sixty-pound audition bag, your purse, and your overcoat into the room for safety's sake. Your audition has gone brilliantly. But back in the hallway, as you sit down to change into your street shoes, you realize that you left your music in the audition room. Oh, no! Ask the monitor if he can retrieve it for you in between auditions. No problem!

A lot of "psyching out" tends to go on in the hallways outside of audition rooms. This is unfair and pretty stupid all around—two actors of the same type may be attempting a form of psychological warfare on each other and may not even be up for the same role!

The theatre can be as cutthroat as any competitive sport and, although it may *appear* true that only the strongest survive, *I* still feel that in the long run it's much better to have friends than enemies. The most pleasant audition (and the most pleasant world, as a matter of fact) is one where people show some consideration toward each other.

So, here are some behavioral suggestions.

- Avoid anything but the lightest of friendly conversations. If you meet a friend or two, suggest that you meet later. Or save your more serious conversation until after you've all auditioned and can move away from the other people.
- Don't get involved in a long listing of your recent credits—this can come off like bragging, and it's possible that you may come up against someone who insists on proving that his credits are more impressive than your own.
- Don't get involved in discussions about what you're going to do for the audition. Keep your trade secrets private.
- Don't warm up, vocalize, or practice your song. Do that someplace outside of the building—like at home.
- If you've been given some sides to study, work on them silently. If you feel you *must* work on them aloud, move far

"I haven't seen you since those *hate*ful auditions. Well, unlike you *I* got the job. I quit that turkey before it even opened. You should be *glad* they didn't like you! What are you singing? Oh, you can *probably* carry that off even though it's usually sung by a different type. But it's *soooo* hard to get it to work and you know Jerry Schliblitz is in there and he *hates* that song. *Everybody* hates that song. Have you dyed your hair? No, well for some reason you're looking *much* better than you have recently, although . . . What? Aren't these the auditions for "Benjy: The Musical"? Oh, well, they should be seeing me for anything they're seeing you for, but I better go to the "Benjy" call. Great to see you! Blah blah blah blah blah blah blah . . ."

enough away from other people so that you don't disturb their preparation.

The time you spend in the hallway prior to your audition is your time to prepare. Use it well. Don't waste it gabbing or trying to destroy someone else's audition. Take that moment to focus on what you are going to be doing and what you are planning to accomplish.

Hey, No Talking!

Here's something that will happen from time to time at your auditions. It's distracting, it's irritating, and it's rude, but right in the middle of your song, you're going to notice that a conversation has begun behind the table. You may lose your concentration, or some part of your mind may start worrying about the horrible things you imagine they're saying about you. Don't let this happen. Don't lose your focus. And realize that in most cases they are trying to figure out how to get the most out of your audition. They could be talking about

- What else they need. Should they ask for an up-tempo? Should they stop you and ask for something more appropriate?
- Whether they should be considering you for a different role.
- Whether they should just ask you to come to the callbacks without asking for anything else.
- How good you are!

The fact that this discussion takes place while you are trying to perform is once again because of the excessive time constraints of the audition process. They really can't afford the time to wait until you're done, have the discussion, and *then* wait for whatever needs to be done to follow up on whatever it was they were discussing.

Callbacks

If you've done a great job *and* you suit the needs of the project (and they like *you*), then it would be logical for you to get a callback. At this point, you'll probably be asked to prepare and read some *sides* (short selections from the play, chosen because a particular character is featured) and possibly a song or two from the show.

Learn this material well. Get very comfortable with it. Many actors I know learn the scenes well enough to be "off-book" (they don't need the script). However, because of the added pressure of the audition itself, it's recommended that, even if you have learned the material by heart, you hold the pages anyway. It's best to keep the sides with you, at least for comfort.

If you are asked to learn a song from the show and

- **the show has been recorded,** you could check out what the cast album sounds like. It's also advisable to spend some time with a pianist to find out what the accompaniment sounds like.

- **the show is brand new,** you may be provided with a demo recording of the material in addition to lead sheets or piano/vocal music. If the printed music differs in some way from the demo, then you should spend time with a pianist to find out what you may hear at the audition.
- **you are provided with just some sheet music, and there is no recording available,** you will have to proceed just as you would in learning any other music (e.g., if you generally work with a coach or accompanist, you'll have to hire one for this learning process).

You'll notice that for all three of the above possibilities I have suggested that you work with an accompanist. A callback is a time when making the investment in a rehearsal pianist is an even more valid expense than at earlier stages. (You can look at it this way: at this point, the chances of your recouping your investment are proportionately greater than earlier on. If, for example, one hundred people were originally seen for the role, then, in a strictly mathematical sense, you had a one in one hundred chance of landing the part. If they're only seeing ten people at the callback, your chances are ten times better, or one in ten, of getting the job—and being paid enough to recover the expense of hiring the accompanist.)

If you haven't been asked to prepare anything special, then you should sing what you sang originally. After all, your performance of it was one of the reasons you got the callback in the first place. But, as always, make sure you prepare some additional material in case they decide they want to hear something else. I've been at auditions where, after the actor has been given no specific request prior to the callback, someone says just as the actor opens his mouth, "Oh, could you sing something different?"

Many actors feel that it's also important that you wear the same outfit to the callback that you wore to the original audition. The theory is that it helps remind the people behind the table of who the actor is and why he was called back. There is also a little bit of a feeling, perhaps, that this outfit contributed to getting the callback or was somehow lucky the first time out. Many's the time Sarah has complained: "Oh, no. Another callback. I'm going to have to hand wash this dress again!"

On some occasions you may be invited to audition for your first time during the callback sessions (perhaps because the casting people believe that you are right enough for the role to have you skip the initial screening auditions, or you're too big a star, or

First Audition   268th Callback

just because they've decided to add more people at the last minute). You must realize that this puts you at a little bit of a disadvantage. If there is special material required (songs or monologues), the actors who are being called back will very likely have had a longer time to prepare their material. Make sure you give this material extra attention—the auditors will not be making any allowances for the difference in time.

Curtain Call

Learn to enjoy your auditions. You'll have to suffer through them for the rest of your career. Even the biggest stars have to at least go in and read a role so that the creative team can be absolutely sure of them. Once you realize that auditions have much in common with performances—which is, presumably, what you want to be doing—you may be able to actually find some pleasure in them.

Observe the effects of your auditions. Keep a log of all your auditions, noting the material you performed, any comments or responses you received, and how you felt about what you did. Try to track the effectiveness of your material, your dress, your attitude, and your state of mind. You should come up with questions like the following:

- Does one song always get a lot of compliments but you never get cast? Try to figure out what that means: Is the song upstaging you? Do you need to replace it?
- Why did the song that is always so effective break down today? Was it an inept accompanist? Were you not paying attention? Was everyone suffering from low blood sugar?
- You were practically in tears from a bad experience with the public transportation system and a song you've never felt totally right about suddenly went brilliantly. Why? Can you figure out a way to recapture that?

In addition, this log should include a list of who you auditioned for; how you heard about the audition, or who sent you out for it; where the auditions where held; and comments (i.e., "Mace Ihvego, the director, was there. He behaved abominably, making nasty comments about my dress. I hope I never have to audition for him again," or, "At Nine of Us Studios—boy, those padded walls can suck your voice right away!").

It can be very scary doing a newly prepared piece of material for the first time publicly. Find yourself a safe place to develop and work on new material. Audition classes that focus on establishing a repertoire are good places to do this work. (Sarah spent every Wednesday night for years at a class like this where she tried out material and perfected songs that she still uses.)

Auditioning is an art, not a science. People are flighty, unpredictable creatures and there are too many people involved in the audition process to be able to predict their decisions with any kind of assurance. In the right time and place, and with the right people, *anything* can work. In the end you must learn how to use and *trust* your instincts. With experience, the solutions that are specifically appropriate for you will become more obvious.

What differentiates a great actor from a mediocre one, or even two great actors from each other, is the choices they make instinctively and the way they act upon those instincts. Experience will introduce you to the people, the places, the attitudes, and the obstacles you will face in your auditions. Your instincts will tell you what is ultimately right.

There is the oft-told story of the young man who has been granted an audition with Richard Rodgers. Since the young man is known for his comic talents, he decides to take the humorous approach, and he assiduously prepares to sing "Oklahoma"—in Hebrew. He goes to some experts to get an accurate translation, and works with the best coaches of singing in Hebrew he can find. Weeks and weeks of constant effort go into the preparation for this one comic moment. He can already hear the peals of laughter and can visualize his triumph—the signing of the contract, wonderful, fascinating meals with the great composer, and universally positive reviews. All leading to a major film career and a weekly network sitcom.

The day of the audition rolls around, and with great excitement, the young man takes the stage.

"What are you going to sing, young man?"

"I'd prefer to surprise you, if that's okay."

"Well, if you must . . ."

The young man cues the accompanist to begin and does his number to stony silence.

"Thanks, but I've heard that one before," says Mr. Rodgers.

Robert Michael Baker tells the story of a horrendous series of callbacks. He was being seen for the lead in a production of *America's Sweetheart,* a musical version of the life of Al Capone. The people could just not seem to make up their minds and Rob knew it was because he looked a little too young for the role. This was to be the seventh callback, but they promised it would be the last.

So, he went to a friend of his, a professional makeup artist who did a serious job on him: dyed his hair black, slicked it back, gave him jowls, and aged and darkened his eyes. He then put on a big pegged suit padded to add some pudginess, a tie with a diamond stickpin, a pair of highly polished Italian shoes, some rings (including a diamond pinky ring, of course), some sunglasses, and a fedora. On his shoulders he placed an overcoat complete with fur collar. Then he went out and got $3,000 in cash which he made into a roll and stuffed into his pocket.

When his name was called, he kicked the door open. It slammed into the wall with a tremendous bang and he stormed into the room. Ignoring all attempts at conversation, he walked up to the table, tossed the roll down and said, in his finest mobsterese, "Ah right. Let's quit fookin' around. I wan' da goddamn show."

His performance was a big hit. The people behind the table went nuts. He sang and read the scenes and then sang some more and read some more scenes. Then he picked up his money and left.

He didn't get the job. They still thought he looked too young.

On the other hand, sometimes really going for it can get more positive results.

My dear friend Laurent Giroux (who was a leading dancer for Bob Fosse for many years and has managed to make the transition from dancer to principal actor) was called in to audition for the role of Herod in the recent national tour of *Jesus Christ Superstar.* He had auditioned for the same role for a regional theatre a year or so earlier and had had no luck.

He woke up on the day of the audition feeling very brave and thinking, "What the heck. These people are from L.A., they don't know who I am, and I'll probably never see them again anyway." So, he put on a net T-shirt, and cut the cheeks out of an old pair of jeans and put them on, sans underwear. Over this he put on a full-length leather coat.

He entered the room very seriously, walked up to the pianist and instructed her not to play a note until he told her to, walked to the opposite end of the room from the casting table, and just stood there. Eventually the people behind the table settled down enough to realize that there was someone in the room and no singing was going on. Once he knew that he had their attention, he casually strolled toward the table while undoing his coat.

Someone behind the table joked, "Oh, what's he gonna do a strip for us?"

Larry tossed his coat down at their feet, lay down on it and proceeded to do what he calls "a horrible, sleazy rendition" of "Herod's Song," finished the number, picked up the coat, turned away (his naked butt a mere five feet from the producer's nose), heard some strangled gasping sounds, and walked out of the room.

The casting director tore out of the room after him and brought him back. Could he do a few dance steps for them? No problem.

The choreographer asked, "Could you make that last leap a little higher?"

"Not in these pants."

"Well, there's so little left to those pants, why not just take them off?"

Larry said, "Not without dinner."

He got the job.

Break a leg!

Appendix A: The Eight-Week Audition Book

F or the actor just starting out in the audition world, one of the greatest handicaps can be a lack of repertoire. Also, while they may have a relatively thick book of audition material, many young actors have a tendency to overspecialize—to emphasize a particular type of musical theatre repertoire, e.g., contemporary pop. My audition classes were designed to remedy this situation.

What follows is a short course outline which can help you develop a nice, full, and varied audition book. For each category you should try to learn two contrasting songs: a fast one (up-tempo, patter, etc.) and a slow one (ballad, torch, etc.). The listed writers are suggestions only and are not meant to limit your choices. The writers are not in any order of preference, and a writer's inclusion in this list is not to be taken as an endorsement of quality. Make your own judgments.

You're on your own as far as finding the actual material. The research element is an important part of the discovery process. The more extensive and wide-ranging your search, the more interesting your material will be and the more likely it is you will discover songs that are perfectly suited to your talents.

Although a complete examination of the correct way to develop a song is beyond the scope of this book, here are some quick thoughts about how you might go about learning the songs:

- Take a week or two to learn each song.
- Before you bother with the tune, learn the lyrics as mono-logues. Work on them from an actor's standpoint exclusively: context, setting, subtext, emotional view, etc. Only when you feel comfortable with your acting choices should you move on to learning the melody. Incorporate what you've learned from your monologue work into your sung performance. Don't think of the melody as a restriction to the acting, but as a support.
- Once you've learned the basics for one category and are mov-ing on to the next, continue to review and work on the songs you've previously learned. Continue to refine and make dis-coveries about each piece.
- Don't worry too much about staging. Let the movement emerge from the acting viewpoint. (My students have told me about a particular audition technique teacher who espouses the use of a very rigid form of staging for each and every number. I've seen the results of this and it looks more like basic training than theatre.)

1. The Classic Musical Comedy: Through the 1930s
Musical Theatre from 1910 through 1940, the early Broadway years.
George Gershwin
Jerome Kern
Early Irving Berlin
Early Cole Porter
Rodgers & Hart
Dietz & Schwartz
Jimmy McHugh
Vincent Youmans
Harry Warren
British Music Hall

2. The Golden Age of Musical Comedy: The 1940s and 1950s
   Don't forget the possibilities of movie musicals.
   > Late Cole Porter
   > Alec Wilder
   > Rodgers & Hammerstein
   > American Kurt Weill
   > Vernon Duke
   > Martin & Blane
   > Burton Lane
   > Frank Loesser
   > Lerner & Loewe
   > Harold Arlen

3. Extreme Legit
   Classical music. More difficult material from outside of musical comedy.
   > Opera
   >> Bizet, Puccini, Verdi, Mozart, Britten, Menotti, Adams, Corigliano
   > Oratorio
   >> Handel, Orff, Haydn, Bach
   > Operetta
   >> Romberg, Herbert, Gilbert & Sullivan, Strauss
   > Art songs
   >> Copland, Barber, John Duke, Ives, Diamond, Weisgall, Rorem, Ricky Ian Gordon

4. Standards & Jazz
   Nontheatrical material. But give it the actor's touch.
   > Johnny Mercer
   > John Green
   > Jimmy Van Heusen
   > Hoagy Carmichael
   > Duke Ellington
   > Billy Strayhorn
   > Django Reinhardt

5. Musical Theatre #1: 1960s and later
   The modern era (but not too contemporary, that's coming later)
   > Jule Styne
   > Jerry Herman
   > Kander & Ebb
   > Harnich & Bock
   > Charles Strouse
   > Cy Coleman
   > Schmidt & Jones
   > Maltby & Shire

6. Musical Theater #2: The Rough Stuff
   More difficult musical theatre pieces.
   > Stephen Sondheim
   > German Period Kurt Weill (with Brecht or Eisner) in translation or not
   > Marc Blitzstein
   > Leonard Bernstein
   > Jerome Moross
   > Stanley Silverman
   > Michael John LaChiusa

7. Rock, Rock & Roll, Folk, and Country & Western
   Go for nontheatre music here. I don't think you need a list of writers.

8. Theatre Pop or Cabaret/Specialty Songs
   Okay, now you can go all-out contemporary.
   > Andrew Lloyd Webber
   > Stephen Schwartz
   > William Finn
   > Stephen Flaherty
   > Galt Macdermott
   > Alan Menken
   > Marvin Hamlisch
   > Tom Lehrer

Appendix B: What Have You Done?

W ell, just who am I, anyway? I have been called a "musical handyman." I have played skillions of auditions: non-Equity, dinner theatre, regional, cabaret, cruise ship, pop and Rock and Roll, off-off-Broadway, off-Broadway, Broadway, opera, revues, previews, workshop, and showcase. I have been a musical director and/or conductor for: *Annie 2* and *Arthur* (Goodspeed Opera House), *Pageant* (The Blue Angel), *Johnny Pye and the Foolkiller* (George St. Playhouse and Lambs Theater), *Up Against It* (The Public Theater), *Gifts of the Magi* (Lambs Theater), *Possessed—The Dracula Musical* (George St. Playhouse), *Tales of Tinseltown* (Musical Theater Works and George St. Playhouse), *Starting Here, Starting Now* (Main St. Theater), among many others. I have been vocal arranger for many of the above. I have been arranger/orchestrator for many of the above, as well as for *Godspell* (1988 off-Broadway revival, Lambs Theater—for which I was also musical director/conductor), *The "No-Frills" Revue* (Musical Theater Works and The Cherry Lane), *The Hits and the Ms.'s* (Rainbow and Stars—for which I was also musical director), *The Summer Winds* (The Naked Angels—in which I also played the onstage pianist), *Guilt Without Sex* (Marilyn Sokol's one-woman show), among many others. I have done big-band arrangements, vocal-group arrangements, choral arrangements, orchestral arrangements. I have coached hundreds of singers, actors, and musicians. I have taught piano, theory, history of music, vocal techniques, repertoire, and audition techniques around the country. I have appeared as computer music consultant on many shows and on several feature films. I have worked as a music copyist for Broadway (*Caroline or Change*, *Spring Awakening*, and *Spider-Man*, among many others), off-Broadway, regional theatre, and film. I have cowritten manuals for music software. I have written dozens of incidental scores for plays, short films and TV, including *Action Painting* (American Theater of Actors), *Vatzlav* (National Theater of Woodbee), *The Disposal* (Jan Hus Theater), *Faces of God* (Artpark), *The Wake-up Call* (award-winning short film), and others. I have written (with both Karen deMauro and the students of participating schools) dozens of children's musicals. And I have composed musicals with Sarah as bookwriter/lyricist, including *The Library*, *The Audition*, *C'est la vie*, *Rappaccini's Daughter*, and *Men and Angels* (formerly *Chamberlain: A Civil War Romance*). With Mark Harelik as bookwriter, we wrote *The Immigrant*, which appeared off-Broadway (and for which I received a Drama Desk nomination). We're currently at work on a new project with D.W. Gregory as bookwriter. And I can often be found playing piano in Sarah's backup band, *The Steve Alper Quartet*, and keyboards with *The Lifesize Gorgeous Cocktails*.

I can be reached via the Internet at: NEXT@knappalper.com.

Index